Michael Bell
Space Replaces Us
Essays and Projects on the City

MW01155780

Michael Bell

Space Replaces Us
Essays and Projects
on the City

With postscripts by Sanford Kwinter and Steven Holl

THE MONACELLI PRESS

This book reflects the influence of many colleagues and friends. In New York and at Columbia, Bernard Tschumi created a situation with new challenges and goals; his support made this project possible. Laurie Hawkinson, Reinhold Martin, Mark Wigley, and Gwendolyn Wright also gave tremendous support. Steven Holl, Kenneth Frampton, Toshiko Mori, Jorge Silvetti, and Stan Allen have been a continual source of critical inspiration. Terence Riley, Aaron Betsky, and Michael Hays all sustained my enthusiasm with their own work and with the new opportunities they provided. Stanley Saitowitz and Antonio Lao influenced my work at its earliest stages. Mark Wamble opened a new view of the city, as did Albert Pope and Sanford Kwinter. Scott Marble has been a great critic and friend, as has Mark Rakatansky. Nothing would have been possible without Kelly Ishida's support. Sze Tsung Leong was my collaborator on *Slow Space*, and his influence shows here. Karen Hsu and Alice Chung have made this a beautiful and intricate book. As editor, Noel Millea brought incredible precision and insight. Trevor Atwell was the managing editor and research assistant for the production phase; he gave the project its initial clarity. With their talent and care, Andrea Monfried and Gianfranco Monacelli have made three books possible. So many people who have worked with me on the projects should be credited, especially Thomas Long, John Mueller, Anthony Burke, Todd Vanvarick, Emily Todd, Rosanne Haggerty, and Mardie Oakes—as should the many students who have shared their work with me. And Francesca Segrè inspired me to keep going when I might have hesitated.

Finally, this book is for my brothers, who explore the world, and my parents, who are always reaching and learning.

First published in the United States of America in 2004 by

The Monacelli Press, Inc.

902 Broadway, New York, New York 10010.

Copyright © 2004 The Monacelli Press, Inc.

All rights reserved under International and Pan-American Copyright Conventions. No part of this book may be reproduced or utilized in any form or by any means, electronic or mechanical, including photocopying, recording, or by any information storage and retrieval system, without permission in writing from the publisher. Inquiries should be sent to The Monacelli Press, Inc.

Library of Congress Cataloging-in-Publication Data

Bell, Michael (Michael J.)

Michael Bell : space replaces us : essays and projects on the city /

with postscripts by Sanford Kwinter and Steven Holl.

p. cm.

ISBN 1-58093-131-6

1. Bell, Michael (Michael J.). 2. Architecture—United States—20th century—Designs and plans.

3. Architecture—United States—21st century—Designs and plans. 4. Architecture—Mathematics.

I. Kwinter, Sanford. II. Holl, Steven. III. Title.

NA737.B42A4 2004

720'.92—dc22   2004008086

Printed and bound in Italy

Designed by Omnivore, Alice Chung and Karen Hsu

Photography by Caroline Dechaine (130, 169), Bjorn Gudbrandsen (166), Deron Neblett (101, 118, 177),

and Benjamin Thorne (78–81, 84–85, 98–99, 102–3)

7   INTRODUCTION

8   Blue House

16   Berlin (Topological) Stoa

22   Double Dihedral House

32   Vallori Plastici

38   House Inside Out: Space Replaces Us

40   Mathematics Day Care Center

49   HAVING HEARD MATHEMATICS: THE TOPOLOGIES OF BOXING

66   Duration House

78   Endspace: Michael Bell and Hans Hofmann

86   Chrome House

98   16 Houses: Owning a House in the City

104   Glass House @ 2 Degrees

117   EYES IN THE HEAT: RSE

128   Stateless Housing

146   Stations House

156   Binocular House

167   STILL NEW YORK CITY

178   EXTENSIVE URBANISM / SANFORD KWINTER

180   TOPOLOGIES OF MICHAEL BELL / STEVEN HOLL

183   PROJECT CREDITS

INTRODUCTION

FIG 1 Houston, 1998. Postwar city: The tools architects have inherited from foundational postwar critics and practices struggle to provide direction in the milieu of the contemporary city. Streamlined and produced with relentless efficiency as a vectoral process, this city has been presumed by many prominent urban theorists to supersede the local acts of architects and architecture.

Michael Bell: Space Replaces Us collects work produced in San Francisco, Houston, and New York between 1988 and 2004. The three essays—"Having Heard Mathematics: The Topologies of Boxing," "Eyes in the Heat: RSE," and "Still New York City"—represent the adjustment of literal and theoretical foundations as the work engaged new sites and territories. In each city, teaching positions anchored this practice. Berkeley, Rice, and Columbia provided more than an academic base; they also offered colleagues whose work was deeply influential and often done in tandem with my own.

The work in this volume conflates two mathematics projects. The first is one of vision and pictorial space as it relates to form (properties of depth, volume, mass, transparency) and figure, and to a standing and perhaps latent humanist subject. The second is that of an operational mathematics of formalization rather than form, a technical optics of material attributes that reveals a molecular frontier concurrent with the numeric prospects of macrofinancial spaces: mass production, standardization, labor mechanisms, and organizations of money over time, the extra-urban dimensions of an economic geography.

Space Replaces Us describes the late modern city, its temporal movements as well as its local and stilled components, and the inhabitants who are often distanced from the creation of the territories they inhabit. Mathematics here is a geometric problem both of minor architectural dimensions and vectors (planar spaces, reduced systems of linearity, and forms of assembly) and of infrastructural, technological, and financial processes—temporal mechanisms that often outmode and outmaneuver architecture and its subjects' local prospects. Postwar cities such as Houston and metropolitan New York are characterized as emblematic of a now ubiquitous United States urbanism whose formal and architectural attributes have become increasingly fragmented and visually inchoate as its trade, labor, financial, media, and production systems have become mathematically unified and self-perpetuating.

Architecture as a small-scale legal component of the city is posited here as an agent of retroactive coherence. As a participant in the great milieu of managerial systems, it provides a lens and intuiting device for comprehending illusive and temporary processes that precipitate the construction of the city. Architecture's political and social agency—its ability to participate in the construction of an urban subject—finds its potency in an enzymatic role. The otherness of the late modern city and its self-regulation subsists in a conflation of perceptual and technical mathematics. Architectural work recovers immanent movements in the stillness of distance; latent procedural histories of legislative policy, capital investment, and speed are reinhabited by an architecture that slows these processes to a threshold of comprehension.

Blue House

Client William and Anita Bell **Site** St. Mary's County, Maryland
Date of Design 1988–90 **Status** Designed **Budget** $150,000

The Blue House was designed to occupy two acres at the junction of the Potomac and St. Mary's rivers in historic St. Mary's County, Maryland. Access to the house requires visitors to traverse a five-hundred-acre farm before reaching the river's edge. The design of this small twelve-hundred-square-foot house was driven by two major concerns, each of which corresponded to issues of theory and design that were ascendant in the late 1980s. The first was an inquiry into architectural typology; the Blue House was derived from a transformation of historically significant regional plans and details. The second was an inquiry into emergent ideas of architectural space in relation to topology. (These same themes form the basis of "Having Heard Mathematics: The Topologies of Boxing," presented later in this book.) The goal was to produce a house that was regionally and historically based, but also contemporary in its spatial inquiry.

The Blue House is organized around a central oculus, and a sleeve- or tube-shaped hallway connects the two major components of the structure. It is, in effect, a continuous surface that folds in on itself like a Mobius strip. The spatial continuity was intended to question the place of the inhabitant amid architectural histories, and the house was organized by function to abet this reading of space. Living spaces are in the main two-story volume, and the thirty-five-foot-long horizontal band of the cruciform forms the bedroom. The two volumes of the bathrooms mimic the twin chimneys typical in the region.

Although the project was not constructed, the model and drawings were purchased for the permanent collection of the San Francisco Museum of Modern Art.

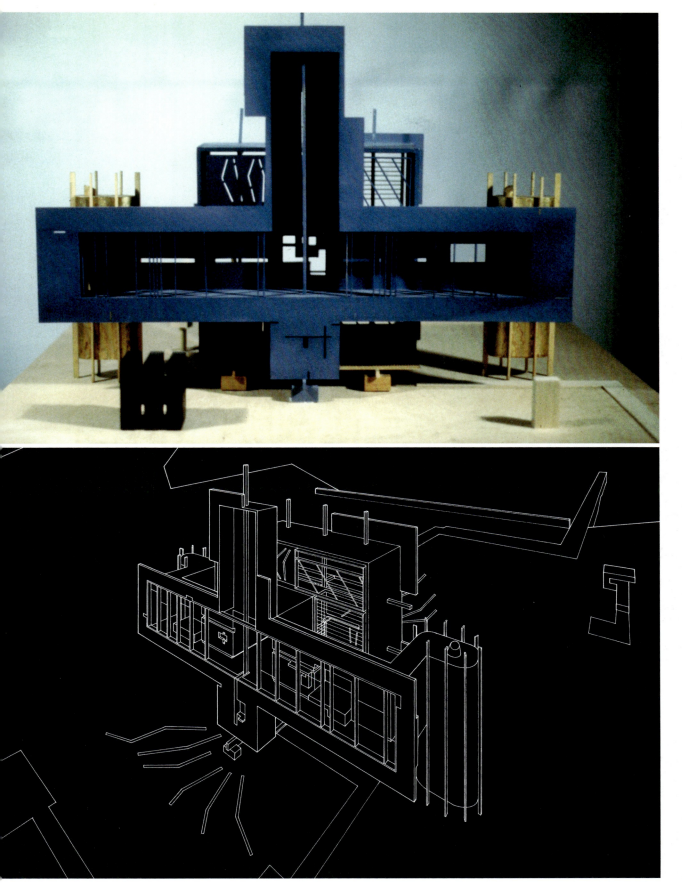

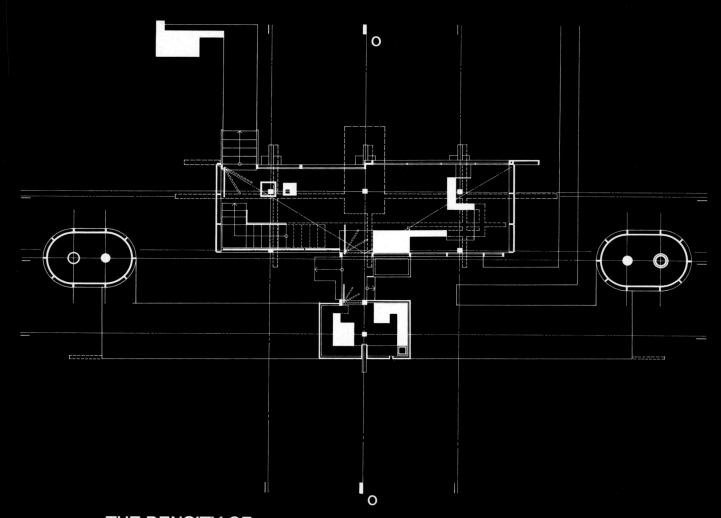

**THE DENSITY OF
ATMOSPHERE TO HAVE
1 A VISCOUS
CONSISTENCY.**

8

4

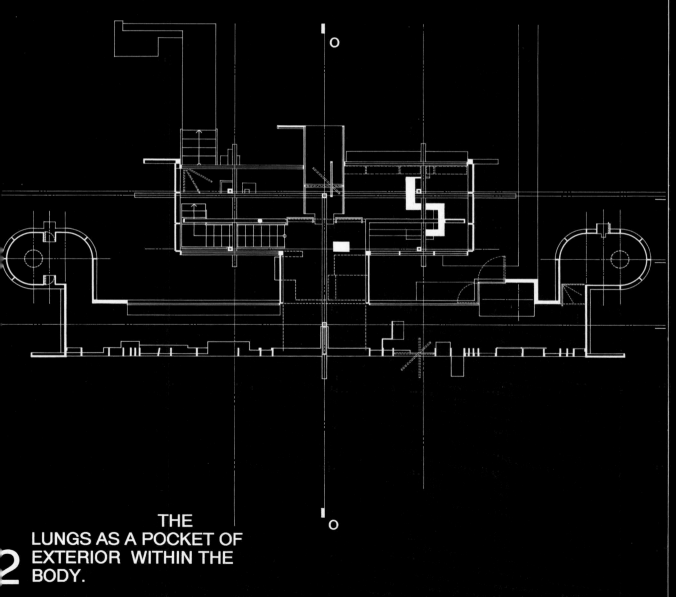

O

O

**THE
LUNGS AS A POCKET OF
EXTERIOR WITHIN THE
BODY.**

2

Site/Type

Many of the Blue House's details are derived from local typologies in the historic tidewater region of the Chesapeake Bay. The facade is a version of Chinese Chippendale, a term used to describe the ornamental rails common in the area, which are said to have been fabricated by a talented woodworker who escaped from prison. The facade's diagonal patterns were extrapolated to serve as a pictorial device that recalls Sol LeWitt's wall drawings.

The Bedroom Spans the Oculus

Bathrooms are on either side of span, and the kitchen connects to the main volume through an outside porch or "curtain."

Blue House Plan

The plan was influenced by Bond Castle, built in nearby Calvert County around 1670, on property originally owned by Sir Cecil Calvert.

Figure–Field/Site

The idea of a third figure-ground condition situated between the possible inversions of figure as positive and ground as negative drives the relation of building and site in the works included in this book. In plan and elevation, they suggest another possibility, that of a space turned inside out, or a void within a void. The works were developed for actual sites; the figure-ground work addresses literal as well as phenomenal readings. By avoiding a retreat to linguistic or semiotic critiques of site and region, it is hoped that they may reveal the pathos of site and place in their plastic qualities. The work of several painters and architects was essential to this study. Prior to undertaking these projects, I spent a year of research at the archives of Theo Van Doesberg, Adolf Loos, and Le Corbusier. The paintings of Robert Slutzky, shown in 1984 at the Modernism Gallery in San Francisco and published in the essay "Color/Structure/Painting" written with Joan Ockman, were also influential.

Bodiless Space

1 A white-hot void
2 A volume removed
3 The space of the subject is collapsed
4 The foreground screen in Raphael's *Freeing of Saint Peter* as a precursor to Mondrian's *New York City*, in which colored bars span rather than divide the surface
5 Giuseppe Terragni's Casa Rustici: syncopation induced by the absent plane

Color

1 Blue Walls: the walls are voided; their surface is that of the atmosphere
2 Color mediates the density of a mass or volume

Architecture is culture, not a mirror or sign of culture.

Plastic Density

1 Plasticity: atmospheric and volumetric density, depicted and recognized at the surface of a solid
2 Plasticity depleted: the equalization of atmospheric and volumetric density at the surface of a solid; the surface collapses; a simultaneous implosion and explosion

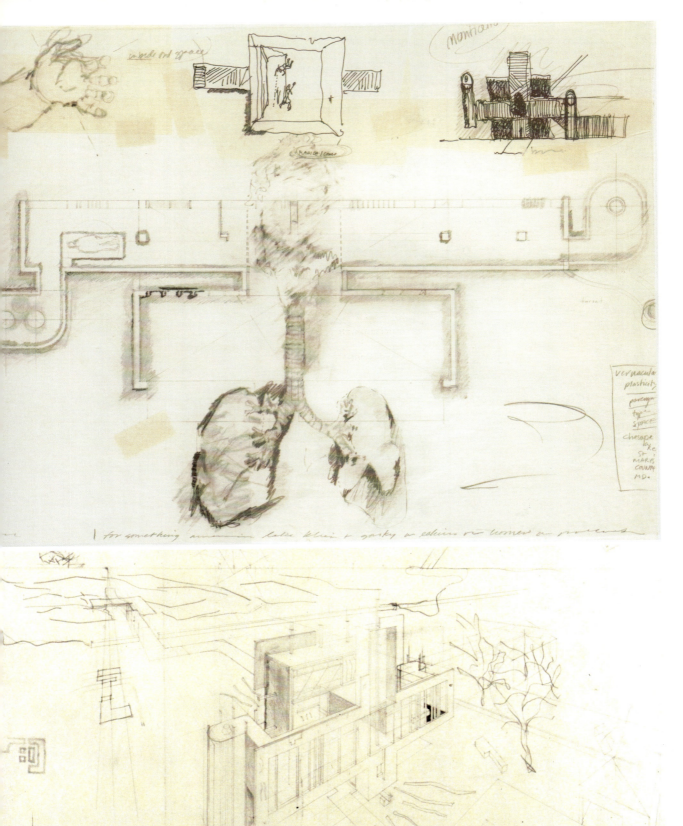

Berlin (Topological) Stoa

Client AEDES Gallery, Berlin   **Site** No Man's Land, Berlin
Date of Design 1988   **Status** Designed   **Budget** $1.5 million

The dimensions and proportions of the Berlin Stoa—designed for a 1988 exhibition on the future of Berlin—were transcribed from the Stoa of Attalos, which stood from approximately 150 BC until AD 267 and took its name from Attalos II, king of Pergamon. In its simplest form, the long, shedlike building, which the Greeks called a "stoa" and the Romans a "porticus," consisted of a roof supported by solid walls on three sides and a row of columns in front. Such a structure involved a minimum of outlay and provided shelter, while permitting the movement of air so welcome in summer. Stoas were commonly found in sanctuaries and marketplaces.

A team of six architects collaborated on the urban design proposal; each architect was also responsible for the design of a component building situated according to a collaborative urban planning goal. The project became a testing ground for ideas concerning architecture and the city.

Berlin Is a City Divided

What was once a single city with a center is now two cities divided by a wall. In this urban design project, the wall with its barbed-wire cornice is transformed—divided down its center, then dragged across No Man's Land like a rake erasing the past. A neutral zone is established and two Berlin walls are created, along with a new city center, a site for new architecture. Building types are scattered throughout the beltlike courtyard that traces its way through Berlin. Topological buildings, such as the new stoa, and typological buildings transformed by the new space face one another, redefining themselves in relation to the others. The inevitability of the historic city grid, the perimeter block, and its associated planning logic gives way to a continuous park, a new habitable boulevard. Like the Blue House, the Topological Stoa is an uninterrupted surface that folds in on itself to form an ambiguous interior and exterior space. It is derived from and anticipates its urban location.

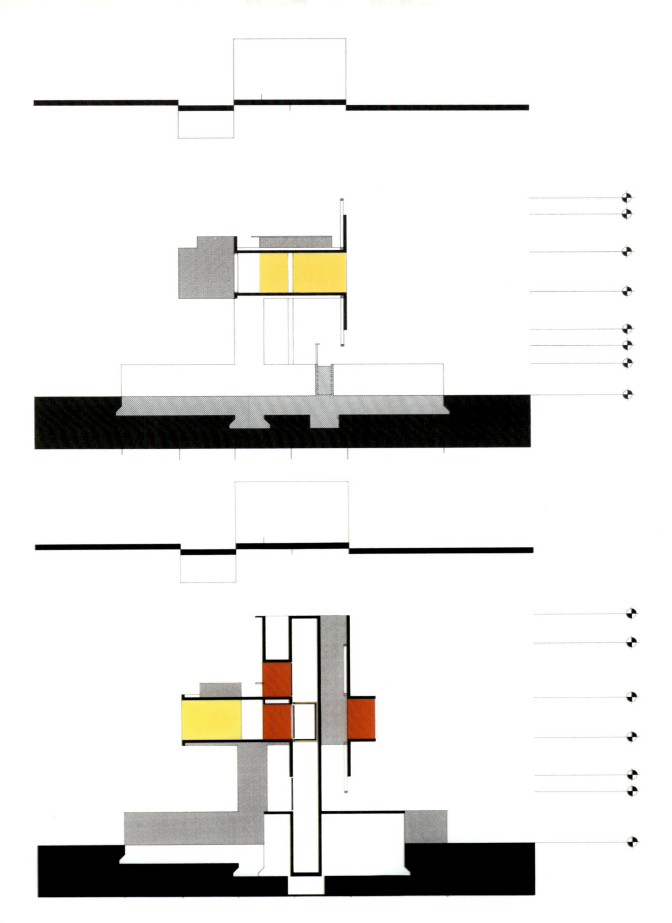

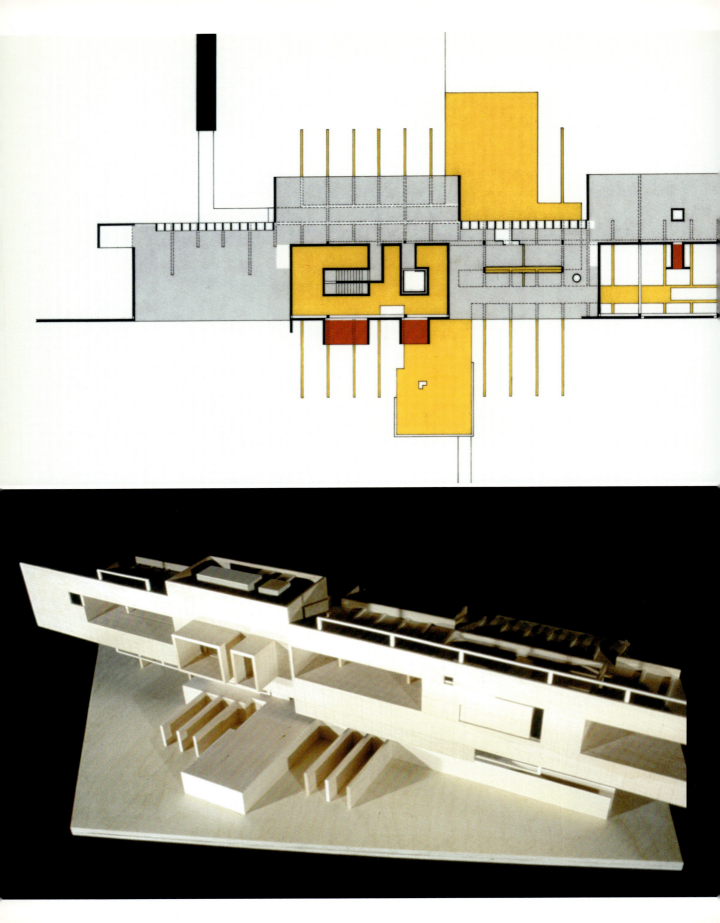

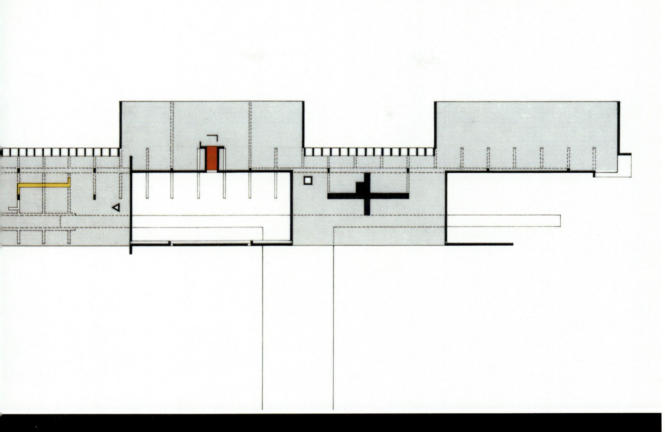

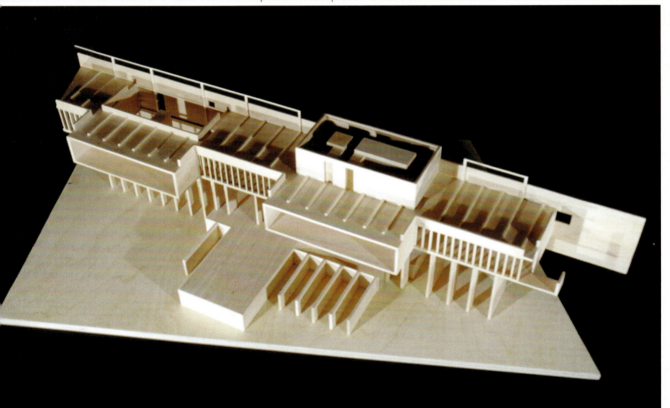

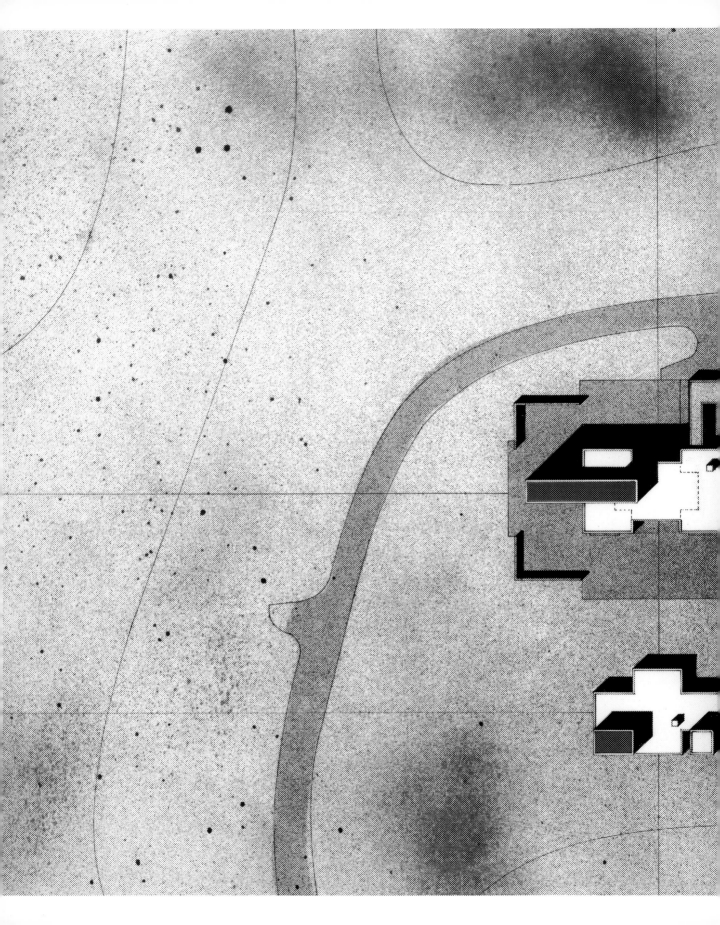

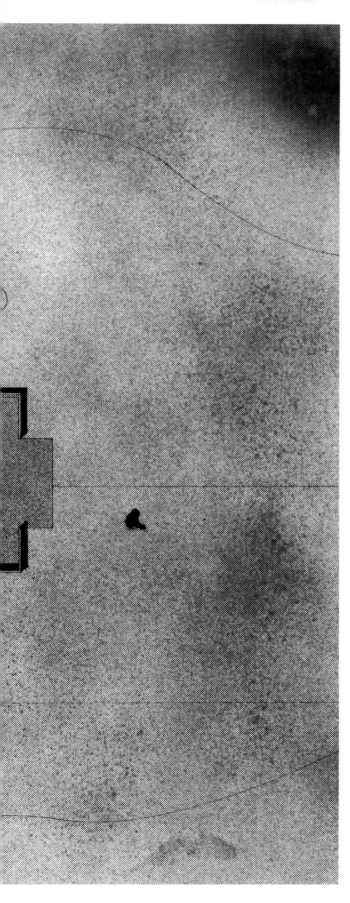

Double Dihedral House

Client Dr. David Lyman **Site** La Cienega, New Mexico
Date of Design 1991–93 **Status** Designed **Budget** $450,000

A house and a gallery for an art collector on four acres of desert near Santa Fe, the Double Dihedral House is simply constructed and composed of elemental planes and primary colors saturated and deepened with black. The program called for one bedroom, two galleries, a reading room, and a small library. The name of the project refers to the occupant as a standing subject; space is organized to reveal depth as well as flatness, and to allow one's gaze to penetrate the entire spatial composition.

A cruciform volume is framed and unframed in the two structures, which are situated opposite one another; each is constituted in reference to its paired other. The frames are quite literal, both in plan and elevation. Upon arrival, the visitor faces four black-framed layers of glass. The trajectory of vision stops momentarily at the first frame, seeking the implied surface, before falling further through the syncopated layers of the other frames. Eventually, the gaze focuses not on the building or the frame but on the unanchored space of the landscape beyond. Under such circumstances, the originative quality of perspectival space fails to provide the footing upon which to survey the Cartesian field.

The relationship of perceiving subject and perceived object is here turned inside out; the hegemony of perspective's constructed subject and its fixed basin is overcome. Through these frames, the visual trajectory turns the space of the building inside out. The roof and floor are cut away to reveal the interior, which is rendered as an outside to its adjacent space.

The model and drawings of the house were purchased by the San Francisco Museum of Modern Art for its permanent collection.

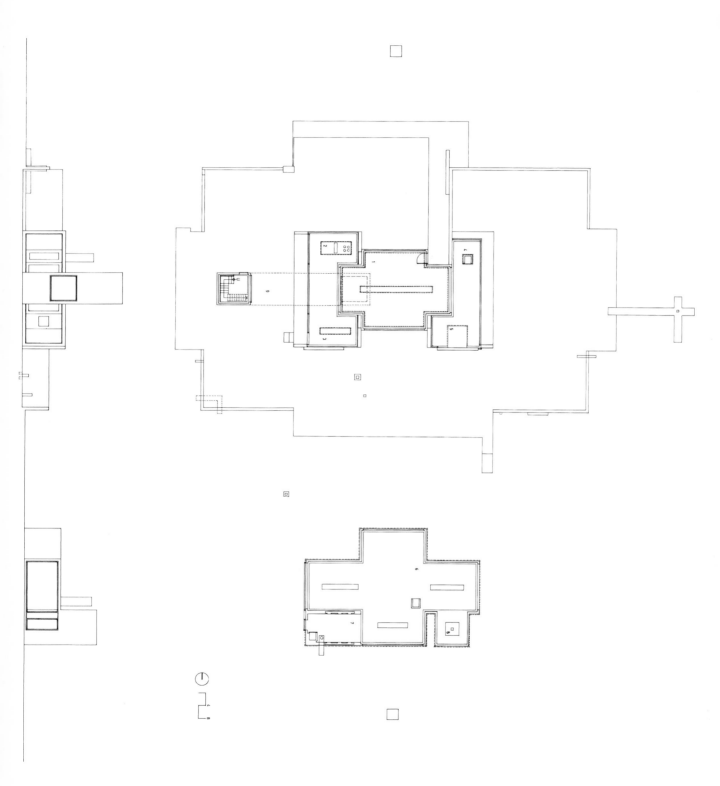

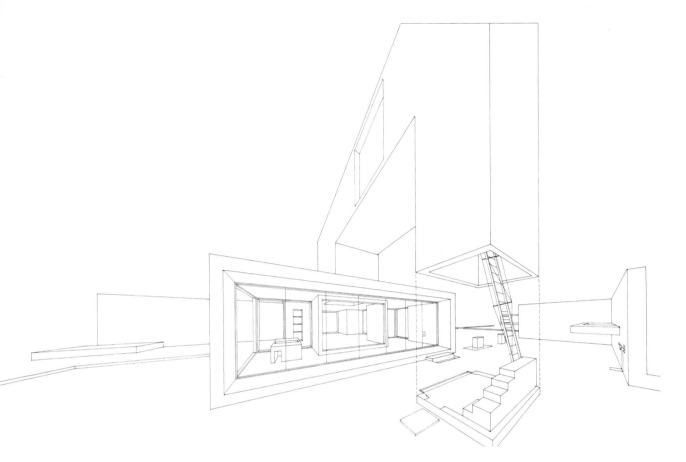

Site Plan

Each structure contains a
central gallery; the north
building contains a bedroom
and a kitchen, the south a
library and a reading room.
Construction is in poured
concrete.

Mimicry and Legendary
Psychasthenia

In the essay "Mimicry and
Legendary Psychasthenia,"
Roger Callois proposes that it
is an organism's ability to dis-
tinguish itself from space
that allows it to form a coher-
ent concept of self or personality.[1] That distinction
between the self and space,
however, is not easily
defined. In the Double Dihedral House, the originative
quality of perspectival space
fails to provide the footing
upon which to survey the
Cartesian field. This failure
also subsequently under-
mines the subject as the origin of space. According to
Callois, "We are allowed to
know, as we should, that
nature is everywhere the
same . . . then the body sepa-
rates itself from thought, the
individual breaks the bound-
ary of his skin and occupies
the other side of his senses.
He tries to look at himself
from any point whatever in
space. He feels himself
becoming space, dark space
where things cannot be put."

1 Roger Callois, "Mimicry
and Legendary Psychasthe-
nia," in *October: The First
Decade*, ed. Rosalind Krauss,
Douglas Crimp, Joan Copjec,
Annette Michelson
(Cambridge, MA: MIT Press,
1987), 70.

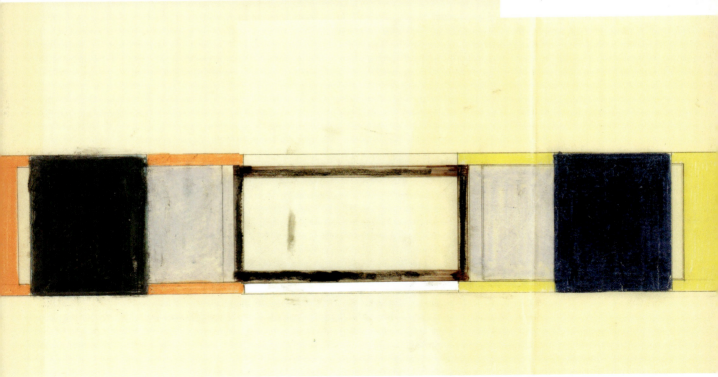

Notes on the Collapse of Plastic Space

Rosalind Krauss and Robert Slutzky both suggest that the frame of a picture provides a reciprocal supportive reaction to that which it contains. Krauss's frame supports the dissipating body in the Man Ray photomontage *Monument to de Sade*. In her essay "The Photographic Condition of Surrealism," she writes, "Two further aspects of this image bespeak the structural reciprocity between frame and image, container and contained. The lighting of the . . . subject is such that the physical density drains off the body as it moves from the center of the image, so that by the time one's gaze approaches the margins, flesh has become so generalized and flattened as to be assimilated into the printed page. Given this threat of dissipation of physical substance, the frame is experienced as shoring up the collapsing structure . . . and guaranteeing its density."[1] In his essay "Aqueous Humor," Slutzky's frame provides the container that allows his reading of a dense "gelatinous" cubist space.[2] For both critics, it is fair to say that a reciprocal plastic relationship exists between the frame and its subject; they are mutually interpolative.

Krauss's Man Ray loads the frame; the subject, on the verge of complete dissolution, is shored up before a final disappearance. Certainly Le Corbusier's boxer, filtered through the above scenarios, must be an aqueous being, a swimmer in a porous and viscous metropolitan match ring. The question that arises then is of unloading the frame—relieving the pressure, so to speak, or curtailing the dialectic relation of frame and subject. In Krauss's scenario, would the anatomy completely dissipate if the frame were expanded or removed? And in Slutzky's case, would the dense space of cubism be possible without the transformative and dialectic mechanics that assured the virtuosity of their architect? One way or the other, there still remains the prospect of a very interesting exploration of the qualities of an architectural and, ultimately, urban space, which seem to have much to do with our time and the plasticity of our spaces. Which plastic possibilities emerge even within the slightest precursory exploration: an unframed space, an unframed subject, thin rather than thick space, a nonplastic milieu?

1 Rosalind Krauss, "The Photographic Condition of Surrealism," in *October: The First Decade*, ed. Rosalind Krauss, Douglas Crimp, Joan Copjec, Annette Michelson (Cambridge, MA: MIT Press, 1987), 174.
2 Robert Slutzky, "Acqueous Humor," *Oppositions* 15–16: 94.

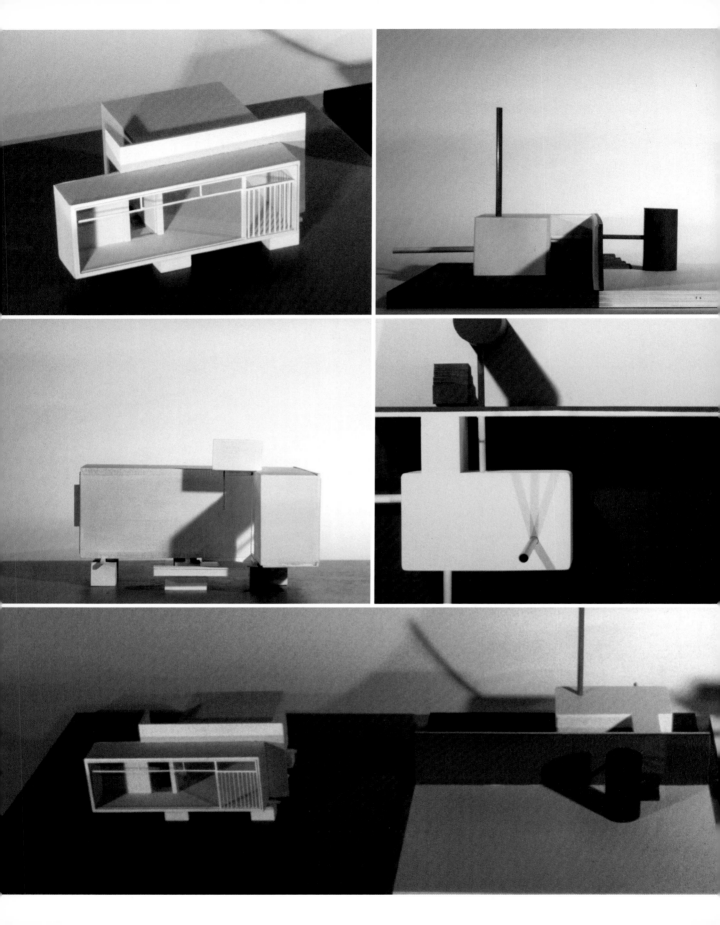

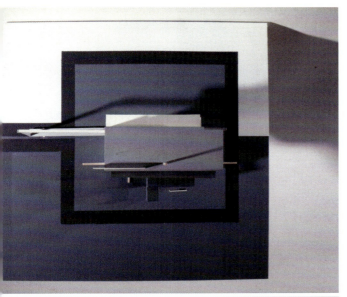

Vallori Plastici

Client Barbara Kelly **Site** Columbia, Maryland
Date of Design 1992 **Status** Designed **Budget** $125,000

The name Vallori Plastici was taken from the title of a journal to which the painter Giorgio de Chirico contributed. Prior to 1920, De Chirico's work frequently portrayed urban spaces that were occupied by a lone, shadowy subject and were defined more by shadow than figure. De Chirico's subjects provided a context in which to imagine a space where daily life could be revealed against an architecture whose plastic presence was palpable but remote. These three studies for a minimal or one-room house were done for a client who initially wished to renovate an existing house in a suburb of Washington, D.C. As the project progressed, it became clear that the new building would serve as a separate private space, adjacent to the domestic life of the existing house but apart from it. The first proposal emphasized shape and color. The second—the Torus House or Court House—offered a succession of spaces that led through the house. The final proposal—the J-Shaped Glass House—used steel and glass as both surface and structure. In all three proposals, the houses were a form of domestic life and architectural still life.

Vallori Plastici 1: Color-fields
Each of these proposals was for a studio at the rear of the existing house. The studies were undertaken prior to designing the client's project in an attempt to isolate a series of spatial relationships that might be used in the three final projects.

These three proposals represent an attempt to establish a series of plastic or mechanical techniques that could be understood to deplete the body's plastic presence in a way that provided some durational autonomy to the landscape, its architecture, and its inhabitants.

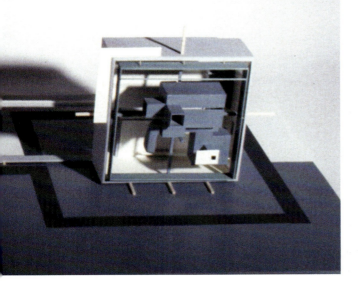

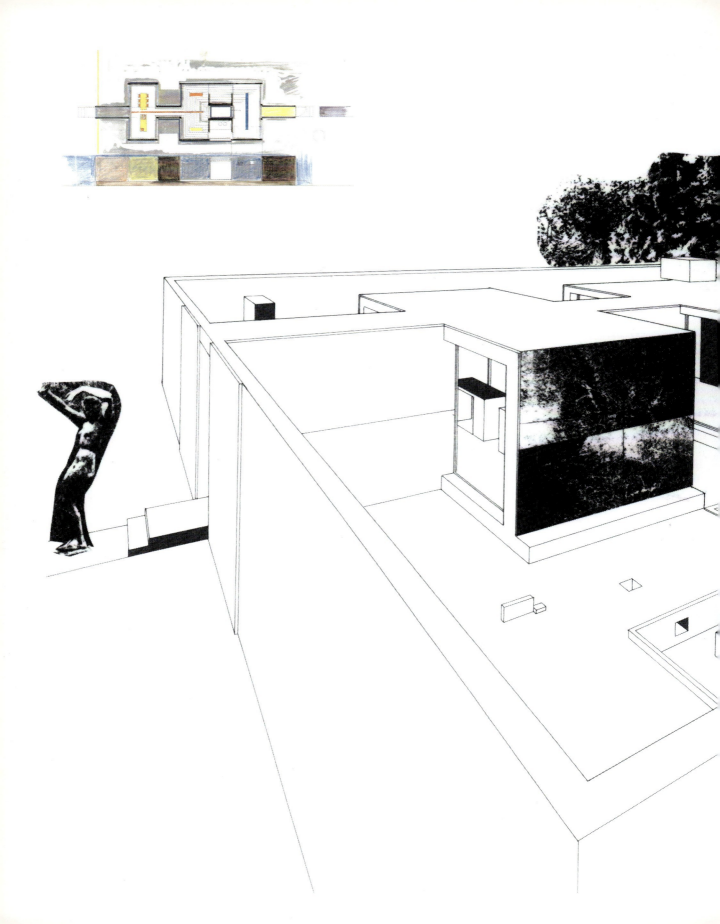

Vallori Plastici 2: Torus, or Court, House

Three chambers form an axial promenade, each dedicated to a particular program. A courtyard surrounds the dwelling and creates an ambiguous negative space. A deep bath is formed in the central court, making a torus-shaped space in the main body of the house.

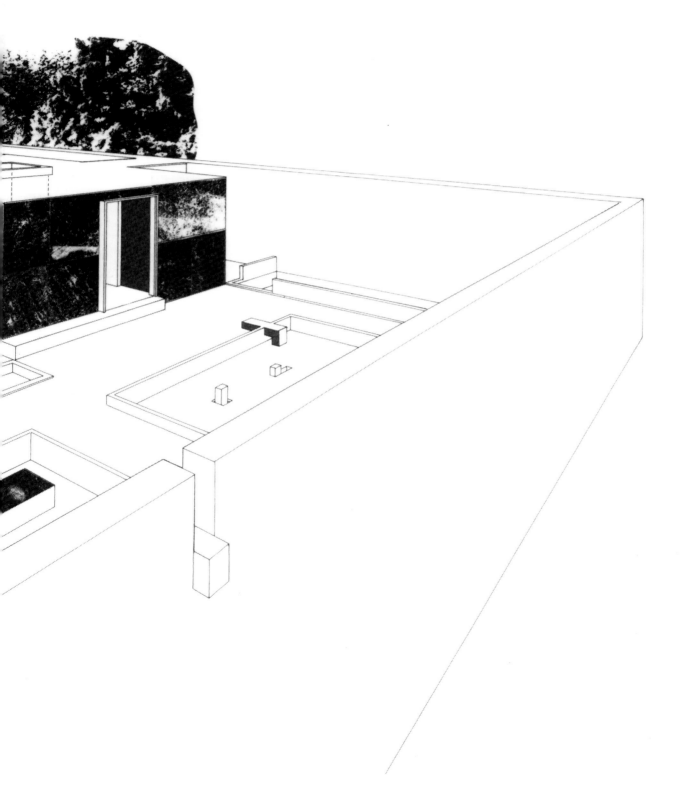

Vallori Plastici 3: J-Shaped Glass House

The J-shaped configuration of the plan sets up a dual vista across the interior and exterior space. The idea is modest in its application but is derived from Michael Heizer's *Double Negative* and Robert Smithson's *Spiral Jetty*. The subject is metaphorically displaced by the twin towers—the bath and the kitchen—and placed outside of space to witness their exchange. This limited volume offers the clients a liberating expansiveness. The project evolved toward a minimalism that alluded to more than was immediately obvious.

Glass House

The freestanding studio or guesthouse was intended to be a time-out zone, a refuge for a family that owns and operates three businesses and has two young children. The courtyard house, also in this folio, was an earlier proposal.

Surface as Structure

The frame is integral to the surface of the building. Two columns fall inside the space, almost as holes in the continuity of the interior volume. The bathroom and kitchen cores are recessed volumes similarly removed from space. A skin surface may, ambiguously, belong to the edge of mass or the edge of space; if it belongs to space, then the building becomes a void and the other edge of space comes into question.

Construction

Four-inch-square steel sections are attached flush with the top outer edge of the foundation slab and the lower outer edge of the roof slab. The columns are set on a fourteen-foot bay. The windows are framed in a steel flange and project past the surface of the columns. The foundation slab is paved with roman brick; in the bath and kitchen, a reveal is cut in the concrete floor. The towers were designed to be fabricated in brick.

Structure

The frame of the building is attached to the outer edge of the floor plate. The complete building structure and closure occurs at the outermost edge. From inside, the subject reaches for the envelope of closure as if it were the outside surface of space rather than the inside surface of volume.

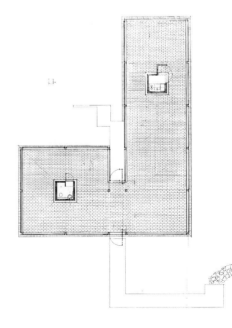

DID YOU EVER DREAM THAT YOU AWOKE TO FIND YOURSELF THE ONLY PERSON LEFT ON THE PLANET. IN MY DREAM EVERYONE IS STILL HERE BUT THEY HAVE ALL GONE INSIDE.

SPACE REPLACES US

OF COURSE I DID NOT REALIZE THIS AT FIRST BUT AFTER I DID I TRIED TO FIND OUT IF AND WHEN ⟶ THEY WERE COMING BACK OUT. SOON I GAVE UP GUESSING AND ⟶ GOT USED TO THE IDEA THAT PEOPLE WERE SOMETHING LIKE A MIRROR AND WITHOUT THEM I COULDN'T SEE A POINT IN SHAVING OR EVEN GETTING DRESSED. SINCE EVERYONE ELSE WAS INSIDE TO STAY I STARTED FEELING AT HOME EVERYWHERE. MY HOUSE LOST ITS CENTRIC PULL AND I STARTED SLEEPING WHEREVER I WANTED. I ONCE PUT MY BED OUT IN THE STREET AND SLEPT WITHOUT COVERS. ANOTHER TIME I PUT MY BED ON A VERY STEEPLY CURVED FREEWAY EXIT RAMP NEAR WHERE I HAD ONCE ALMOST REAR ENDED ANOTHER CAR BECAUSE I CAME UPON IT TOO QUICKLY. MY HOUSE SEEMED LIKE IT HAD BEEN TURNED INSIDE OUT AND I FELT LIKE I WAS EVERYWHERE ALL AT ONCE.

H O U S E   I N S I D E   O U T

USUALLY THOUGH I JUST SLEPT AT HOME IN THE BEDROOM WITH THE WINDOWS SECURED AND DRAPES PULLED AND THE DOOR LOCKED. I GUESS IT WAS JUST FOR OLD TIMES SAKE BUT IT MADE THE ROOM SEEM LIKE ANY POINT ANYWHERE. AT NIGHT I WOULD GO TO SLEEP TRYING TO HOLD THAT THOUGHT WHILE SIMULTANE-OUSLY THINKING OF ALL THE OTHERS IN THERE ROOMS AND THE CONTINUOUS SPACES BETWEEN US.

DURING THE TOPOLOGICAL REVOLUTION OF 1993 MY HOUSE WAS TURNED INSIDE OUT. MY NEIGHBOR'S HOUSES RESISTED BUT THICK GREEN SHRUB-BERY SPROUTED AND BELTED THEM ALL INSIDE TILL THE PHYSICISTS' COULD FIGURE OUT WHAT HAD HAPPENED. I CALLED MY NEIGHBOR ON THE PHONE AND HE TOLD ME WE WERE ABOUT TO ENTER THE REALM OF TRUE MODERNITY BUT UNTIL THEN WE WOULD HAVE TO BE CONTENT TO SPEAK ON THE PHONE. NO ONE WAS COMING OUT PAST THEIR SHRUBS. MY HOUSE DIDN'T HAVE A SHRUB SO I WENT OUT TO SEE WHAT IT WAS LIKE

SPACE REPLACES US
T O P O L O G I C A L   C I T Y / H O U S E

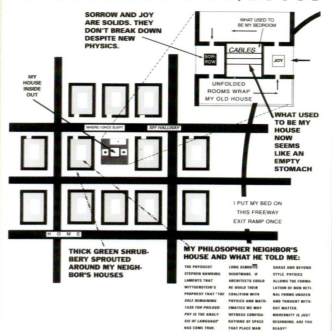

THICK GREEN SHRUB-BERY SPROUTED AROUND MY NEIGH-BOR'S HOUSES

MY PHILOSOPHER NEIGHBOR'S HOUSE AND WHAT HE TOLD ME:

THE PHYSICIST STEPHEN HAWKING LAMENTS THAT WITTGENSTEIN'S PROPHESY THAT *"THE SOLE REMAINING TASK FOR PHILOSO-PHY IS THE ANALY-SIS OF LANGUAGE"* HAS COME TRUE. HENCE OUR CENTURY LONG SEMIOTIC NIGHTMARE. IF ARCHITECTS COULD RE-BUILD THEIR COALITION WITH PHYSICS AND MATH-EMATICS WE MAY WITNESS CONFIGU-RATIONS OF SPACE THAT PLACE MAN OUTSIDE OF LAN-GUAGE AND BEYOND STYLE. PHYSICS ALLOWS THE FORMU-LATION OF NON RETI-NAL FORMS UNSEEN AND UNTHOUGHT WITH-OUT MATTER. MODERNITY IS JUST BEGINNING. ARE YOU READY?

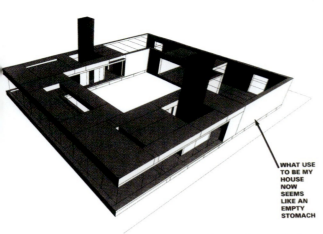

SPACE REPLACES US

WHAT USE TO BE MY HOUSE NOW SEEMS LIKE AN EMPTY STOMACH

OF COURSE I DID NOT REALIZE THIS AT FIRST BUT AFTER I DID I TRIED TO FIND OUT IF AND WHEN THEY THEY WERE COMING BACK OUT. SOON I GAVE UP GUESSING AND AND GOT USED TO THE IDEA THAT PEOPLE WERE SOMETHING LIKE A MIRROR AND WITHOUT THEM I COULDN'T SEE A POINT IN SHAVING OR EVEN GETTING DRESSED. SINCE EVERYONE ELSE WAS INSIDE TO STAY I STARTED FEELING AT HOME EVERYWHERE. MY HOUSE LOST ITS CENTRIC PULL AND I STARTED SLEEPING WHEREVER I WANTED. I ONCE PUT MY BED OUT IN THE STREET AND SLEPT WITHOUT COVERS. ANOTHER TIME I PUT MY BED ON A VERY STEEPLY CURVED FREEWAY EXIT RAMP NEAR WHERE I HAD ONCE ALMOST REAR ENDED ANOTHER CAR BECAUSE I CAME UPON IT TOO QUICKLY. MY HOUSE SEEMED LIKE IT HAD BEEN TURNED INSIDE OUT AND I FELT LIKE I WAS EVERYWHERE ALL AT ONCE.

TOPOLOGICAL

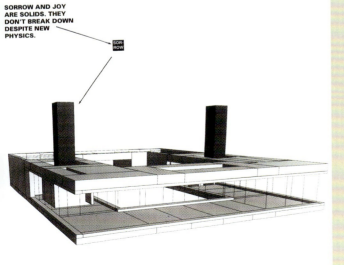

SPACE REPLACES US

CONJECTURE? YES...BUT THE FACTS ACCUMULATE: MIES AND STEPHEN HAWKING EXAMINE THE ARTIFACT AND RECALL BATAILLE'S THE IMPOSSIBLE. THE THIRD MEMBER OF THEIR PARTY - A SOCIAL WORKER REALIZES THAT ECONOMIC TOPOLOGY HAS MADE THIS A TRUE STORY FOR THE HOMELESS ON AMERICAN STREETS

DURING THE TOPOLOGICAL REVOLUTION OF 1993 MY HOUSE WAS TURNED INSIDE OUT. MY NEIGHBOR'S HOUSES RESISTED BUT THICK GREEN SHRUBBERY SPROUTED AND BELTED THEM ALL INSIDE TILL THE PHYSICISTS COULD FIGURE OUT WHAT HAD HAPPENED. I CALLED MY NEIGHBOR ON THE PHONE AND HE TOLD ME WE WERE ABOUT TO ENTER THE REALM OF TRUE MODERNITY BUT UNTIL THEN WE WOULD HAVE TO BE CONTENT TO SPEAK ON THE PHONE. NO ONE WAS COMING OUT PAST THEIR SHRUBS. MY HOUSE DIDN'T HAVE A SHRUB SO I WENT OUT TO SEE WHAT IT WAS LIKE

SORROW AND JOY ARE SOLIDS. THEY DON'T BREAK DOWN DESPITE NEW PHYSICS.

SORROW

CITY/HOUSE

House Inside Out:
Space Replaces Us

Client *Japan Architect* **Date of Design** 1992
Status Unbuilt **Budget** $200,000

This project was created for an annual open competition sponsored by *Japan Architect* magazine. Each year an invited juror sets the parameters and judges this competition, which focuses on themes of housing and domesticity. In 1992, Rem Koolhaas was invited to act as author and jury. In his call for entries, he solicited designs for a "house with no style," encouraging participants not only to avoid "the frivolous and decorative," but also to "avoid all nostalgia, avoid the 50s, avoid the 60s, avoid palm trees, avoid (almost all) angles that are not 90 degrees, avoid color . . ."

This submission proposed that the house be turned inside out and that occupation take place in the city. A torus-shaped space with a glazed front area faces a suburban street; as one progresses through the house, it alternately opens vertically to the sky and horizontally to the landscape. The court is connected to the site with a covered passage. The project is diagrammatic as an architectural proposal; it functions as both architecture and narrative. It won a fourth place—honorable mention prize and was one of sixteen projects recognized out of 732 international submissions.

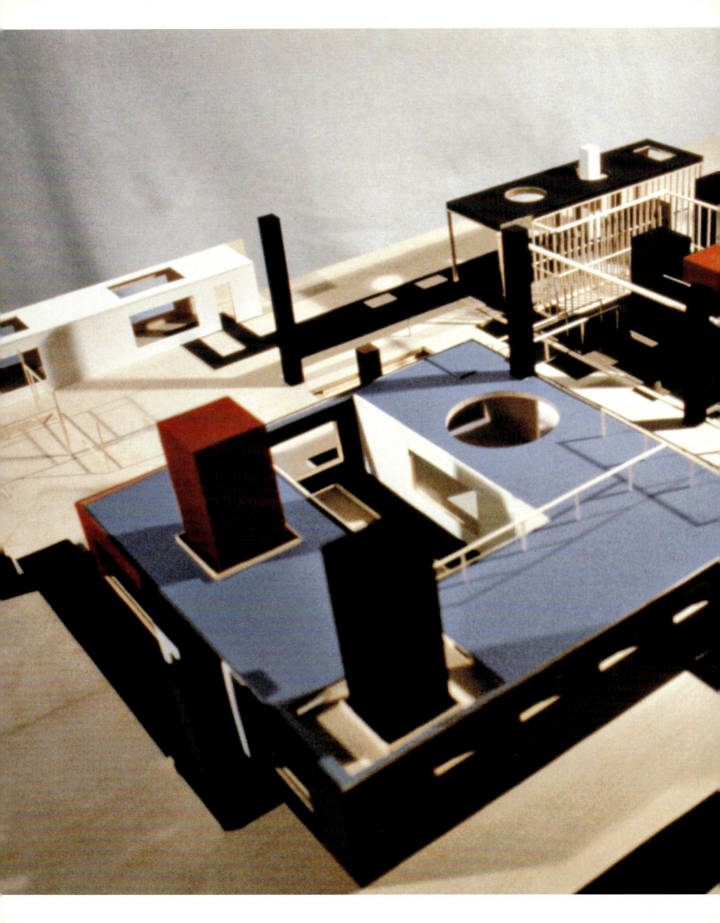

Mathematics Day Care Center

Client Karen Mondanado **Site** Clarksville, Maryland
Date of Design 1992–93 **Status** Designed **Budget** $500,000

After five years in business, having overseen the care of more than a thousand children, the owners of a suburban Maryland day care center decided to move their business to a small site behind a new forty-acre commercial project on the edge of a watershed protected from development by zoning and the Environmental Protection Agency. (The site is located on the outskirts of Columbia, Maryland, a planned community near Washington, D.C.) The clients' foremost concern was creating an environment that would allow children to construct a space for themselves in the city. They were also concerned with how the building might influence the way the children perceived themselves.

The design strategy was to create a building that would contain a sense of immanent time—a building based on ideas of torsion, gravity, and buckling that could provide some new structure of time that might allow children to see the megalopolis in a different way. The day care center is a building that could allow children to make time more plastic.

Model

A small kitchen and cafeteria area occupies a wing of the building. The second-level floor extends to form a roof over the serving counter. Two circular skylights are centered over the counter below. A square peg in a round hole allows for an exhaust vent from the kitchen.

The building faces a playing field with a small bridge that children must cross to reach the entrance. The thin second-floor post-tensioned floor plate is revealed in the elevation. The first-floor glazing system engages the underside of this plate and the sill of the ground-floor slab.

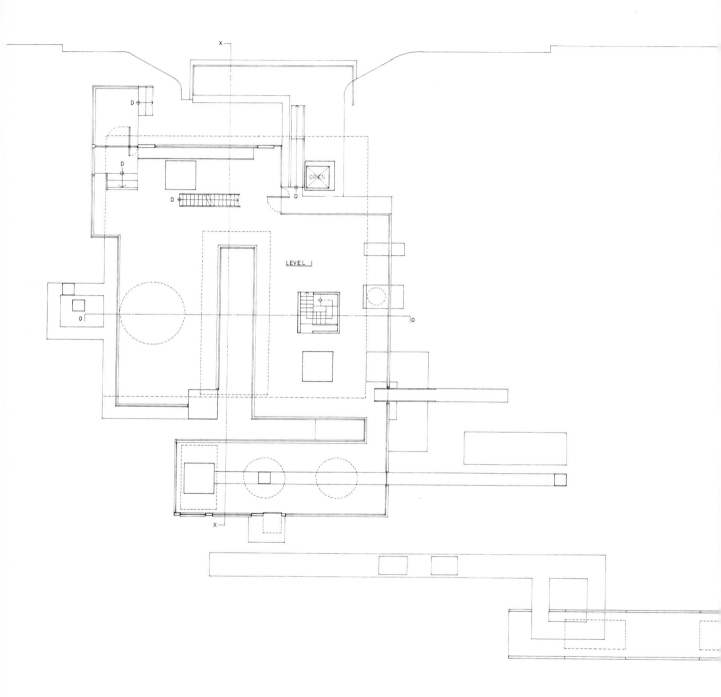

X

D

D

D

D

OPEN

LEVEL I

O

O

X

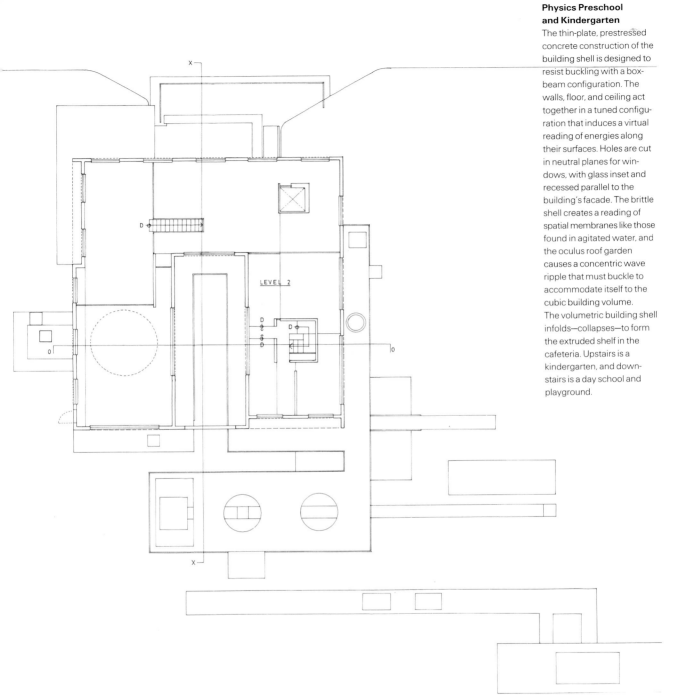

LEVEL 2

Physics Preschool and Kindergarten

The thin-plate, prestressed concrete construction of the building shell is designed to resist buckling with a box-beam configuration. The walls, floor, and ceiling act together in a tuned configuration that induces a virtual reading of energies along their surfaces. Holes are cut in neutral planes for windows, with glass inset and recessed parallel to the building's facade. The brittle shell creates a reading of spatial membranes like those found in agitated water, and the oculus roof garden causes a concentric wave ripple that must buckle to accommodate itself to the cubic building volume. The volumetric building shell infolds—collapses—to form the extruded shelf in the cafeteria. Upstairs is a kindergarten, and downstairs is a day school and playground.

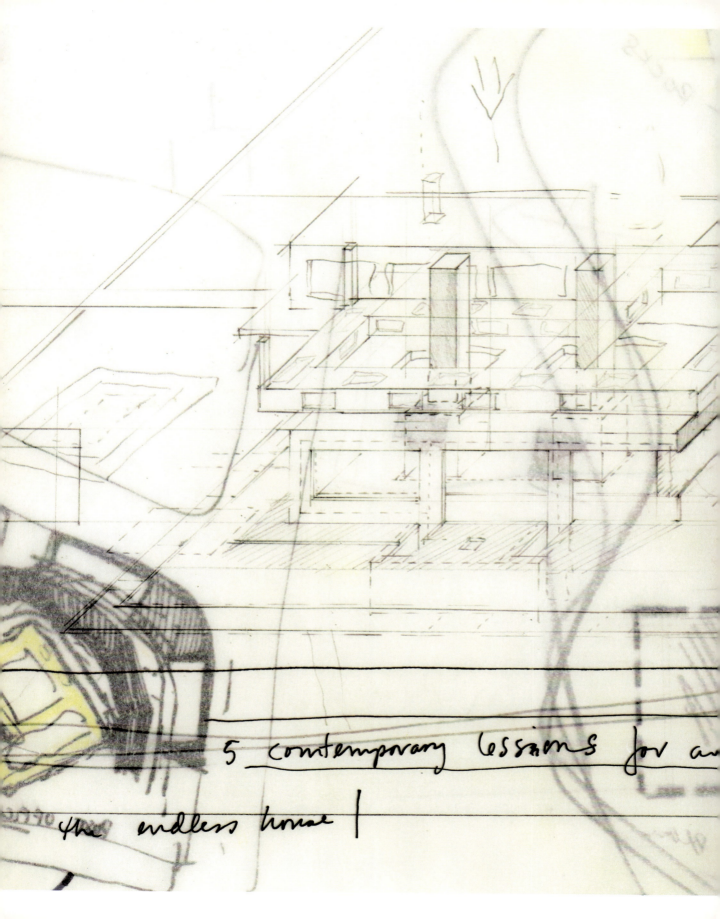

5 contemporary lessons for a

the endless house |

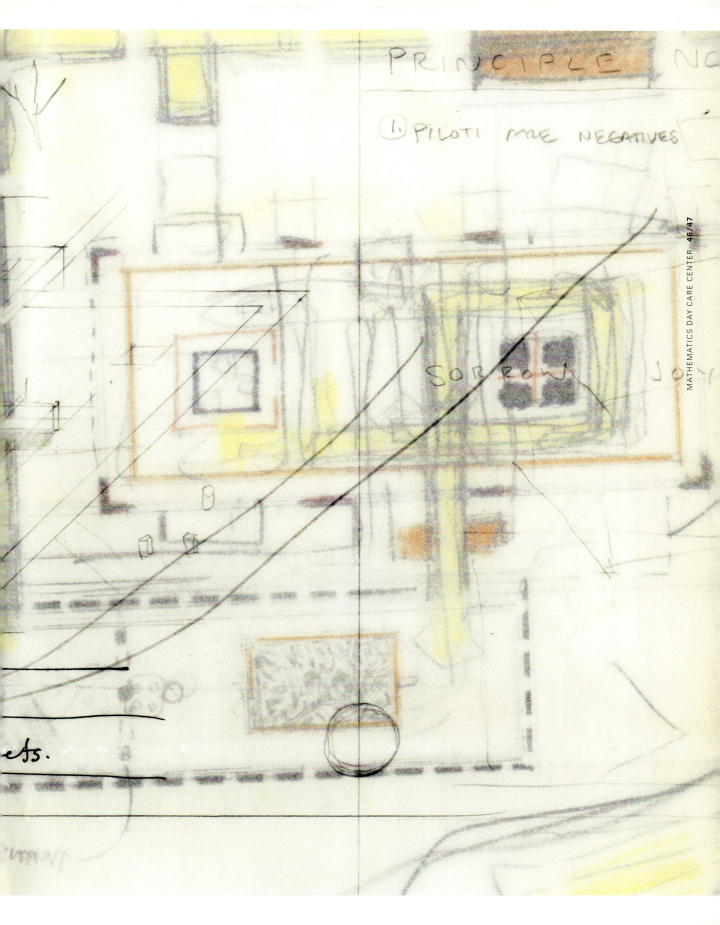

FIG 1 Giuseppe Terragni, Casa Rustici, Milan, Italy, 1933–35
FIG 2 Hoffman Genus 1

1 Norman Bryson, "The Gaze in the Expanded Field," in *Vision and Visuality*, ed. Hal Foster (Seattle: Bay Press, 1988), 87–108.
2 Bryson, "The Gaze in the Expanded Field," 89.
3 Robert Slutzky and Joan Ockman, "Color/Structure/Painting," in *Robert Slutzky: 15 Paintings*, 1980–1984 (San Francisco: Modernism Gallery, 1984), unpaginated. Also contains essays by John Hejduk, Dore Ashton, and Alberto Sartoris.
4 Frank Stella, *Working Space: The Charles Eliot Norton Lectures* (Cambridge, MA: Harvard University Press, 1986), 82*ff.*

Otherness

In his essay "The Gaze in the Expanded Field," Norman Bryson ascertains a subject persecuted at the center of both Jean-Paul Sartre's and Jacques Lacan's accounts of the gaze.[1] Bryson's critique asserts that both Sartre and Lacan retain a conceptual frame that posits a subject as the origin of space even as they reveal that this sovereignty is menaced by the presence of other origins. In Sartre's case this competing origin is another viewing subject, while in Lacan's scenario the subject is challenged by the opaque presence of other inanimate entities, things that "look back."

To illustrate Sartre's theorizing of the gaze, Bryson relies upon a composition by Raphael, *Marriage of the Virgin* (1504), in which he claims that Raphael has annihilated the viewing "subject as center" at the very instance when this subject has taken up the composition's offered station point. The vanishing point of Raphael's composition is portrayed as inextricably bound to the viewpoint; it leads the viewing eye toward what Bryson calls the "drain" or "black hole of otherness placed at the horizontal horizon."[2] Bryson's analysis of the painting reveals an implacable decentering: Raphael's architectural space is one that evades the sovereign occupation of a viewing subject at the crucible of this subject's attempts to occupy the apex of the pictorial field.

Bryson's characterization of the mechanics of this subjectless space bears quite literal similarities to both Frank Stella's critique of Piet Mondrian's *Broadway Boogie Woogie* (1942–43) in his book *Working Space* and to Robert Slutzky's self-defined initiatives in the series of fifteen paintings he completed between 1981 and 1984.[3] The pictorial device that Bryson refers to as a drain or black hole—the vertical white rectangle that composes the door within Raphael's architecture—has a correlative counterpart in both Stella's and Slutzky's pictorial explications. Stella attributes similar subject-annihilating tendencies to the device: "It is here that Mondrian rattles the bones of human configuration for the last time; it is here that the white rectangle steps out of the background landscape into its own space,"[4] he wrote in the transcription of the Charles Eliot Norton Lectures he delivered at Harvard University in 1983 and 1984. Stella depicts two techniques by which Mondrian transformed the reliance of pictorial space upon perspective, especially perspective's regulation of a frontal and positioned subject. Stella claims that the colored bars of Mondrian's late paintings span rather than divide the surface of the compositions and in doing so allow for the emergence of a truly modern pictorial space, a space of abstraction that does not rely on perspective's horizon line or a relative station point. Of the paintings *Victory Boogie Woogie* (1943–44) and *New York City* (1941–42), Stella states that Mondrian had given rise to a background source of light whose progressive emanation allows it to be understood as foreground. Within this foregrounded yet formless atmosphere lies the enunciation of a space secured by Mondrian's "hot blooded structure" and "live-wire armatures," a space capable of providing a freely directionless extensity of shape and duration. Though Stella does not offer this possibility, it seems that Mondrian's white rectangle places itself behind and around its frontal subject.

During the same few years in which Stella delivered his Norton lectures, Robert Slutzky prepared a series of fifteen paintings also dominated by a centralized and usually white square, what Slutzky calls an oculus. The paintings were presented at the Modernism Gallery in San Francisco in 1984 and subsequently published in a monograph that includes an essay entitled

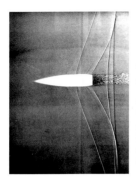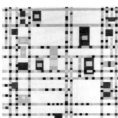

"Color/Structure/Painting," which Slutzky cowrote with Joan Ockman. Slutzky and Ockman referred to this centralized square as the "counter eye in the canvas," an oculus that confronts "the artist and spectator alike." Bryson calls attention to this dynamic with Sartre, whose account of his solitary dominion over a park setting is undermined by the arrival of another person. Bryson cites this scenario in identifying a menaced and decentered subject within Sartre's conception of the gaze. Upon realizing he is not alone, Sartre finds himself occupying a tangential relationship to an other. His vision converges on this other, where he is not and where he cannot be. Slutzky and Ockman ascribe to these fifteen canvases a bit of both Sartre's animate other and Lacan's inanimate things that "look back." Though they do not ascribe to this "counter eye" the explicitly existential aspects of Sartre's tangential subject, Slutzky and Ockman by interpolation instigate a transformation of vision's role in the positioning of the self as both origin of and object within a provisional field. In fact, it is the enframed field that these paintings slowly but surely reconfigure in an increasingly willful compositional process. As the oculus confronts the artist, the artist responds, and one epistemological crisis is undone by another: Slutzky and Ockman state that this oculus turns "space inside-out," and "like a torus-glove" it makes "figure and field ambiguously one." There is no doubt that these plastic mechanics ultimately remain dialectical despite the spatial ambiguity they portend and Slutzky betrays no need to deny the canvas as an originative surface. Like Sartre and Lacan, Slutzky and Ockman still seem to posit their subject, at least momentarily, as the origin of the visual field. Though perhaps his subject-painter is menaced as well, Slutzky's oculus offers an intuitive vantage and grasp of the inferable, a chance to seize and then occupy the composition's topologically transformed space.[5] In this way the dialectic transparency of Slutzky's techniques constitutes a revelation of the enframing device and of the mechanisms of representation. The oculus offers the opportunity to intuit the unframed duration of events. In providing the fixity and frontality that is both learned and reflexively anticipated, Slutzky also provides a comprehension of time as form—this work is representational, even perhaps a model, but it also operates enzymatically in use, or more accurately, under duress. Here it ceases to be a model and becomes a lived experience. Slutzky's paintings offer the opportunity to relinquish form but they also suggest, perhaps fetishistically, that we decline the opportunity. This retaining of distance between viewing subject and perceived world allows for a critical vantage that is ultimately difficult to consider menaced. Slutzky and Ockman may here be understood to provide a pictorial impetus, a visual inducement that forecloses on a final and catastrophic transformation of the pictorial field itself and with it the fixing of a discrete subject and an object. This transformation takes vision irrecoverably past the plastic limits of its learned Cartesian basin and in doing so moves the locus of our cognition onto a dispersed and unfolded field. In this sense Slutzky's work also asks viewers to annihilate their own visual origins and having done so to enter a space of extensivity, a space of uncharted and unanchored movements. To Bryson this type of expanded field results in an alleviation of the conceptual frame retained by Sartre and Lacan. Drawing from the philosophies of Kitaro Nishida and Keiji Nishitani, Bryson notes that it appears as if the frame is "withdrawn." The subject-object dialectic that has been reified within modern practices dissolves in this expansion and the subject no longer posits itself against that which it is not.[6] In

FIG 3 Shock-wave pattern from a projectile at near sonic speed

FIG 4 Piet Mondrian, *Broadway Boogie Woogie*, 1942–43, collection of the Museum of Modern Art

FIG 5 Robert Slutzky, *Untitled C*, 1983

FIG 6 Raphael, *Marriage of the Virgin*, 1504

FIG 7 This model of a Klein bottle belongs to topologist Albert Tucker of Princeton University: nobody will ever see an actual Klein bottle because it exists only in the topologist's imagination; a true Klein bottle passes through itself without creating a hole, a physical impossibility

5 Robert Slutzky suggests that his paintings have topological qualities. They seem to intuit rather than model a particular type of topological form known as a minimal and embedded surface, which is boundaryless and non-self-intersecting. Described in finite terms, a minimal surface is capable of infinite extension without self-intersection. Until recently only three such figures were known: the plane, the catenoid, and the helicoid. Others, such as the Menger sponge and the hypersphere approximate the conditions described. Their lack of boundaries, framing data, and segmentation disallows readings of space that seek distinctions or

edges. Ivars Peterson, *The Mathematical Tourist: Snapshots of Modern Mathematics* (New York: W. H. Freeman & Co., 1988), 56–59.

6 For the sake of clarity, I have attributed the concept of an "expanded" or "withdrawn" frame to Norman Bryson, who actually interpreted earlier work by Kitaro Nishida and Keiji Nishitani. Bryson situates the idea of an "expanded field" within his comparison of Sartre's, Lacan's, and Nishitani's theorizing of the gaze. Bryson, "The Gaze in the Expanded Field," 96–98.

7 Bryson, "The Gaze in the Expanded Field," 100.

8 Bryson, "The Gaze in the Expanded Field," 108.

9 A characterization of space as thin or dissolute is related to a concept of thickened space as presented in another essay by Robert Slutzky, "Aqueous Humor." Slutzky portrayed what he called "a progressive and typically cubist thickening of space" in the late works of Le Corbusier, specifically in the buildings that employed the brise soleil. This thickening of space was generated largely by innovations in the vertical surfaces of Le Corbusier's buildings. "The cubist medium," says Slutzky, "is not one of ethereal clarities, but of dense, gelatinous ambiguities." Cubism, and in Slutzky's

this manner the subject is able to reposition itself as a "being that exists through the existence of everything else in the universal field."[7]

Robert Slutzky's techniques operate within a structure of formalist mechanics; while color and shape modulate depth and Cartesian geometries provide a willful author's heuristic structure, Slutzky pushes each of these dimensions to its extreme, to its plastic limit. The painter speaks of blues that are not quite blue (as Josef Albers might have) and squares that are not quite square. Without this pushing of limits there would be good reason to believe that these techniques are no longer capable of serving as a critical apparatus. The topology of Slutzky's desired transfiguration of pictorial figure and ground presents the means for a significant critical reappraisal and transformation of Cartesian perspective's dominion in the description and regulation of a contemporary and increasingly visual subject. The pervasiveness of new and still predominantly visual computer interfaces is reason enough to continue to consider the ocular an important project, but they are clearly only the most blatant and erotically taunting conscriptions of cognitive vision that constitute daily life.

Slutzky, like Mondrian, seems to have been rattling "the bones of human configuration for the last time." He speaks of unanchoring our contemplative eyes for distant journeys and faraway places, loci of our memories rebirthed." Slutzky's paintings allow for the intuiting rather than the modeling of such a space. As such, these paintings must be understood to be critical; they offer the preservation of an immanence within the represented that could sustain the migratory and lateral passages and cycles of an expanded and authentic life. Bryson's essay concludes with the suggestion that the "real discovery" of his critique of the gaze is that "things we took to be private, secluded, and inward," such as "perception, art, the perception of art in a museum, are created socially. What is at stake is the discovery of a politics of vision."[8]

Within the dissipative and unbounded spaces of such contemporary urban cities as Houston, the idea of a withdrawn or expanded frame seems in some sense ironic.[9] On the plateau of late capitalism's vacated version of the "city," vision is alternatively vast and instrumental.[10] What Martin Heidegger termed the "malice of rage"—an increasing tendency toward nihilism that is endemic to a reification of vision within modernism today—has an odd and complex resonance in the dissolute spaces of sprawling American cities such as Houston. Here the blankness of the white rectangle already predominates both in the vertical and horizontal planes, yet it rarely emerges in clear distinction and it hardly defines a landscape of its own, at least not a sublime landscape. In these cities, television's conscription of vision reigns over the fabrication of a cognitive and social citizen, yet the horizon—the real horizon—of this flat and immense city is literally a 360-degree circle, and its enveloping topology ultimately vanquishes any attempt to demarcate either a station point or origin. Malice is unable to find clear footing, and rage, when it does occur, seems unable to articulate its province and thus unable to sustain prerogatives. The material, labor, and shape of space in these cities, almost exclusively orchestrated within the quadratic equations of capital investment, leave the eye/the subject/the citizen in the devastated scenario of trying to cohere the formed remnants and entropic by-products of a process of clandestine financial machinations. When an expected perspective does occur in the contemporary city it hardly constitutes a hegemonic device but rather a perceived relief. We know

what it is and we probably even realize that it is artificially contrived. On one hand, vision is confiscated by the devices of the media, and on the other it is presented with a vacancy of such shapeless expanse that it is overwhelmed. Either scenario seems to lead toward a constituent humiliation. The white rectangle, Mondrian's sublime device of metropolitan criticism and of negative dwelling, here offers an ironic and suffered respite.[11]

"We are still in the city," states Cacciari in "The Dialectics of the Negative and the Metropolis," "as long as we are in the presence of use values alone, or in the presence of the simple production of the commodity, or if the two instances stand next to each other in a nondialectical relation." We inhabit the metropolis "when production assumes its own social rationale, when it determines the modes of consumption and succeeds in making them function toward the renewal of the cycle." Houston, and indeed most of America's so-called metropolises, demands a renewed characterization of these terms, for one could argue that the distended space of these post-metropolitan cities is nondialectical even as it has succeeded in establishing modes of consumption that are essentially self-sustaining. The blankness of space in these cities seems also to engender a self-sustaining virus, a metabolic mechanism whose undermining presence is assured by managed capital's seeming inability to cohere plastic space. This blankness, a result of capital's desperate need to maximize the vectoral coefficients of production, nonetheless poses its own dialectic traps of rather primitive geometric origin: efficiency of transportation relies on geometric parameters in the production and assembly of contemporary building materials to such an extent that contemporary building techniques are almost incapable of producing truly plastic form or space. Efficiency in the production, sale, and transportation of materials also requires a clandestine, or at least hidden, method of dealing with gravity as it pertains to building design, material configuration, and ultimately to human weight and presence. The discrete nature of architectural practice within these post-metropolitan processes ironically might be understood to offer at least two alternatives, both derived from an engagement of the limits of architecture's professional involvement in urban machinations of finance. The first alternative lies in the "rattling of the bones of human configuration for the last time," in occupying Slutzky's inside-out space. The nihilistic attributes of blankness recede in the expanded field.[12] Having occupied this space, a second alternative emerges based in the activity of a "being that exists through the existence of everything else."[13] If this rattling is incomplete, if a vestige of a frame remains, it seems possible to work within, rather than model, the shapes and processes of the contemporary city itself. In some sense Slutzky's oculus provides the sequel to the texts he wrote with Colin Rowe; the habitation of these spaces might be considered not as the mathematics of, but instead the topology of, the post metropolitan city. It is a topology that must be lived rather than represented. The means of procurement of this lived space, however, must in some way remain visible if such a space is to endow its subject with critical authority.

Giuseppe Terragni: Vision and Duration

The following section presents an analysis of two buildings designed by Giuseppe Terragni in collaboration with Pietro Lingeri during the early 1930s. These two projects, Casa Rustici

paradigm the architecture of Le Corbusier, "savors the water rather than the air." The cubist thickening of space that Slutzky depicts in these works is activated at the periphery of Le Corbusier's late buildings; here Le Corbusier instigates a turbulence that delaminates the otherwise unmitigated flow of space into and around a building mass and volume. At Chandigarh, the brise soleils of the Secretariat, the Palace of Justice, and the Assembly all activate a dramatic alluvial play of space that is perhaps the last great public manifestation of architecture within a vigorous and willful plastic sensibility. Le Corbusier's buildings are both the basin—"the container-like still life"—and the sieve; they operate as enzymatic perturbations in what would otherwise be a placid field. In a sense, they both constitute the field and instigate a reformation of its plastic qualities, a dialectic process but one seemingly without origin. Slutzky's reading of Le Corbusier's thickened space has a correlative antinomy in Rosalind Krauss's analysis of Man Ray's *Monument to De Sade* in the *October* essay "The Photographic Condition of Surrealism." Krauss suggests that the cruciform frame Man Ray has inscribed upon the surface of a photographic print provides a supportive reaction to the figure it contains. She also claims that the cruciform frame drawn on top of the Man Ray photograph shores up an otherwise dissipating body: "The structural reciprocity between frame and image, container and contained . . . The lighting of the buttocks and thighs of the subject is such that the physical density drains off the body as it moves from the center of the image, so that by the time one's gaze approaches the margins, flesh has become so generalized and flattened as to be assimilated into the printed page." But this assimilation is thwarted or held at bay: "Given this threat of dissipation of physical substance, the frame is experienced as shoring up the collapsing structure . . . and guaranteeing its density." In the Krauss and Slutzky critiques, the relationship between the frame and that which it contains defines the plastic qualities of the works. The frame and subject are not independent, and in some way their relationship is organic because they are mutually interpolative; they posit each other in a spontaneously migrating reformation of supporter and supported. Man Ray loads the frame; on the verge of complete dissolution his subject is shored up before final disappearance, yet this

subject also assures the eventual stability of the frame. Le Corbusier's boxer, filtered through Slutzky's scenario, must be an aqueous being—a swimmer in a porous and viscous metropolitan match ring. The question that arises in this context is one of unloading the frame—relieving the pressure or curtailing the interpolative dialectic relationship between frame and subject. In Krauss's scenario, would the anatomy completely dissipate if the frame were expanded or removed? And in Slutzky's case, would the "dense" space of cubism be possible without the transformative and dialectic mechanics that assured the virtuosity of their architect? There remains the prospect of a very interesting search into the qualities of an architectural, and ultimately urban, space of our time.

10 Massimo Cacciari, *Architecture and Nihilism: On the Philosophy of Modern Architecture* (New Haven: Yale University Press, 1993), 7.

11 The reference to negative dwelling is derived from the term *kakania* in Robert Musil's *The Man Without Qualities*. Kakania "was the most progressive State of all; it was the State that was by now acquiescing to its own existence. In it one was negatively free, constantly aware of the inadequate grounds for one's own exis-

tence and lapped by the great fantasy of all that had not happened, or at least had not irrevocably happened, as by the foam of the oceans from which mankind arose." Robert Musil, *The Man Without Qualities*, trans. Eithne Wilkins and Ernst Kaiser (London: Picador, 1979), 34.

12 Bryson, "The Gaze in the Expanded Field," 97. The term *blankness* is a reference to Nishitani; the actual term is *sunyata*. Bryson translates its intended meaning as "radical impermanence."

13 Bryson, "The Gaze in the Expanded Field," 97.

FIGS 8–10 Casa Rustici, 1933–35

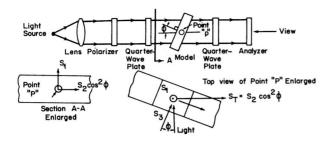

FIG 11 Diagram of the photo-elastic process

(1933–35) and Palazzo Littorio, Scheme A (1934), are characterized by an overt preoccupation with a classicized and monumental frontality. Both projects, however, also offer the potential of a transformed visual field, a field whose edges at times seem alternately expanded or eradicated. The essay's primary interest is the Palazzo Littorio, specifically the photo-elastic, finite-element analysis phase of this project; however, the issues of perspectivalism that this project involves itself in are relevant also to both Casa Rustici and Casa Giuliani-Frigerio (1939–40). Underlying this analysis is the assumption that Palazzo Littorio exemplifies a phase of design in which Terragni and Lingeri effectively separated form from vision and in doing so clarified the spatial potential of material and matter itself; in other words, they bring to a cognitive level an ideal of material duration as a replacement for perspectival relativity. Peter Eisenman's analysis of Casa Giuliani-Frigerio will later be brought to bear on the conception of an unframed and nondialectical, yet still plastic, conception of architectural space, a space that has antecedents in the canonical works of de Stijl architecture and painting.[14]

Eyes in the Heat

The design of Palazzo Littorio was abetted by a series of photo-elastic stress analysis experiments to predict the distribution of stress and strain forces in the surface of the building's cantilevered wall. These experiments were perfected within a general refinement of the principles and mechanics of camera and lens techniques, as well as the chemistry of the photographic process itself. Palazzo Littorio's program, in essence a speaking platform for Mussolini, was to be sustained by the spectacle of the massive cantilever allowed by these experiments. The space of this instrument of political authority was derived from the literally deep and frontalized choreography of a political audience, yet it was also a space of shallow depth developed within the camera and lens techniques of photo-elastic processes. These techniques effectively flattened the actual perspectival depth of the project within the thermodynamics of photographic chemical processes. Palazzo Littorio's perceptual and literal frontality relates it vividly to the string of six apartment houses that Terragni designed with Lingeri in Milan in the early 1930s. The perspectival principles of these works culminate in Casa Rustici, a project that, like Palazzo Littorio, vigorously establishes a planar modulation of depth as it simultaneously threatens its compositional stability.

The frontal arrangement of space in Casa Rustici operates in a manner similar to both Mondrian's work as described by Frank Stella and Robert Slutzky's ocular paintings. Terragni and Lingeri over-dilate the viewing eye; the architects invite the viewing subject to take up the apex of the offered space as they withdraw its authority. The proportion and rhythm of openings in the facade of Casa Rustici sets up a syncopation within the parameters of a field established by the overt frame surrounding the primary facade of the building. Readings of apparently recessive or progressive planar depths are modulated peripherally and centrally in unexpected ways that ultimately undermine the eye's ability to cohere the classicized formal characteristics of the composition. Terragni and Lingeri focus the eye not on the form of the building but on the central space between the two primary masses that house the apartment units. Like Mondrian's bars that Stella claims span rather than divide, the balconies of the Casa Rustici seem to span the voided center of the building. In doing so they give rise to a complex space, a space that cannot be

14 Peter Eisenman, "From Object to Relationship II, Casa Giuliani-Frigerio: Giuseppe Terragni Casa Del Fascio," *Perspecta 13/14*: 36–65. For Eisenman's relation to Terragni, see also Sanford Kwinter, "Challenge Match for the Information Age: Maxwell's Demons and Eisenman's Conventions," *Architecture and Urbanism* (September 1993): 146–49.

FIG 12 Stress concentration factor determined by photo-elasticity

FIG 13 Fringe pattern in disk containing a central hole (load applied at the top and bottom center): Patterns emerge as a result of polarization of light-wave vibrations; the waves vibrate at different magnitudes depending on the stress in the material they pass through or refract from

FIG 14 Photo-elastic stress analysis, circa 1934: a light source is polarized before it reaches the structural model; the camera—the analyzer—records a limited spectrum of light waves and thus is able to reveal a fringe pattern that emulates the stress and strain in the model. Photo-elasticity was the primary method of experimental stress analysis used to determine structural stability during the 1930s. As a form

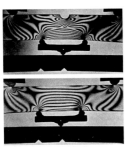    

of finite element-analysis, the photo-elastic process reveals an observable relationship between optical patterns generated within a transparent material—a model—and the eventual behavior of the actual structure under loading. Photo-elastic tests provide a quantitative result: the processes rely on the discretization of both structural mechanics and the optic properties of light within the dialectic of tension and compression. The organization, behavior, and distribution of stresses within the surrogate material used in the modeling are witnessed in the patterns generated as a light is passed through the assembled model. As a control parameter, the light is captured by a camera with a polarizing lens; the polarization reduces the visible spectrum of light waves and delimits the complexity of the revealed stress patterns. The refraction of light waves caused by the material deformation coincides with the primary stress points, and the changes in the velocity of the transmission of light as it passes through these materials reveals a readable pattern. This pattern coincides with the stress distribution in the model and ideally within the materials employed in construction.

read as positive or negative, recessive or progressive, or even as plastic in any traditional sense of the word. It is a space more akin to a vacuum than to a simple absence. The horizontal expanse of the facade establishes a distinct peripheral datum; against this datum it is possible to read flanking window bays as progressive surfaces against a center that appears to be recessive. Yet the readings can be reversed; the light that Stella understood to emanate from the background of Mondrian's composition here forces the eye to relinquish its reliance on any expected background or foreground arrangement of space, thus mandating an abdication of enframement or plastic figuration. The peripheral surface's windows, stacked five floors high, appear oversized as well, an attribute consistent in both Loos and Terragni, as well as in contemporary work by Álvaro Siza and Frank Gehry. While they retain a vestige of the oculus, the windows' expansiveness undermines the progressive reading of the surface; the eye falls deep into them, unable to grasp the distanced ocular frame. These wall surfaces are at once progressive and recessive; against the outer edge of the facade's frame they appear to have receded, yet against the vectoral direction and speed of a frontalized vision they appear progressive. The oculus-window in these surfaces offers the depth-seeking eye a chance to move deeper into space, without offering anything to look at. Recalling Lacan, it also seems here that nothing looks back either. Space seems to replace the other.

The proportion of the windows in the facade of Casa Rustici, however, is sufficient to cause a kind of peripheral delay or momentary pause. We are asked to consider the nature of the oculus and the represented before relinquishing either. This delay, if understood within a model of ballistics, instigates a degree of turbulence: ballistics tests have shown that when a bullet passes through a plane of Plexiglas, it causes a turbulence that is roughly coplanar with the surface of the glass but is derived from the direction, velocity, and shape of the bullet. As the bullet continues its slowed and damaged trajectory, this turbulence models a topology that in effect resolves and describes the catastrophic collaboration of the vectoral and planar dimensions of the experiment's two components. If the geometries of vision were equated with those that describe the movement of the bullet and given a conical form, the topology of the turbulence could be understood to seek the orthogonal building form. As the balcony-bridges span the white-hot void of the building's court, a subjectless court with a glass floor, the eye's ability to hold on to the form of the building and composition must ultimately be intuited rather than represented. The mechanics of the eye are thwarted in this struggle; the eye falls deep into the central space, its speed and directionality damaged by the interaction with the facade, but it is continuous nonetheless. The result is an awareness of the architectural form, presumably of human life, that extends beyond the relativity of the frontal view and the station point. Terragni and Lingeri triangulate the anticipated bipartite relationship of subject and object within a durational field—the Casa Rustici denies both subject and object as origin, positing each as a durational entity within an expanded field.

Palazzo Littorio: Buckling and Immanence

The photo-elastic stress analysis diagrams that accompany the design presented by Terragni and Lingeri for the 1934 Palazzo Littorio competition have garnered little attention and even less inter-

pretation, although they have been published widely.[15] They appear in the Zanichelli monograph on Terragni, in the book *Surface and Symbol* by Thomas Schumacher, and Peter Eisenman certainly will address them in some format in his forthcoming book on Terragni. The reproduction of these images has consistently seemed dutiful rather than enlightening. This claim, however, sets aside Manfredo Tafuri's essay, "Giuseppe Terragni: Subject and Mask." Because Tafuri's explication does not examine the intrinsic properties of the photo-elastic processes,[16] he is forced to reconcile their significance in the design of Palazzo Littorio within the linguistic prerogatives of his own research. Tafuri seems unable to synthesize his linguistic research and his sometimes startling structural and mechanical insights. For example, while Tafuri recognizes that the apparent wall composing the primary facade is actually a "boxlike structure" rather than a wall—a fact that completely changes not only the mechanics of its cantilever but also its ability to "speak," in Tafuri's lexicon—the author still admits that he is unsure why the isostatic lines of the photo-elastic process are represented on the surface of this facade.[17] Tafuri's analysis focuses on the belief that Terragni has reduced these "forces" to an arabesque, a dissolution of an "apodictic word." The following analysis of Palazzo Littorio instead attempts to more completely situate Terragni and Lingeri's ambitions within the techniques of the photo-elastic process itself. In doing so it reveals the building's fabrications of power and political authority, as they are manifested in the realms of optics, perspectivalism, lens and camera mechanisms, chemistry and photo processes, and ultimately in constituent subjectivity.

Photo-elastic Stress Analysis

Photo-elasticity was "the method of experimental stress analysis" during the 1930s.[18] As a form of finite element analysis, the photo-elastic process revealed an observable relationship between optical patterns generated within a transparent material and the distribution of stresses that migrate through the material under loading.[19] The behavior of the material under stress is witnessed in the patterns generated as a polarized light passes through the assembled model. The polarization produces a light whose waves vibrate within a single plane; as a control device, the polarization allows for the discretization of an otherwise infinite number of wave axes. In certain materials, the refraction of this polarized light coincides with the material's primary stress points. Changes in the "velocity of the transmission of light" as it passes through these materials reveal the pattern of stress distribution as it occurs in the model.[20] Since the model stands in for an actual material, the value of these results must be extrapolated in order to be of use. Given the scale of the cantilever that Terragni and Lingeri proposed in Scheme A of what would eventually total three design submissions, it is not surprising that they chose to perform some stress tests in the form of finite element analysis. But why would Terragni and Lingeri choose to use the stress patterns culled from the photo-elastic studies as a primary element in the final design proposal? In the case of Palazzo Littorio, the isostatic lines that depicted the evaluation of stresses in the photo-elastic model were to be traced into the building's facade by steel support cables.

The facade of the proposed speaking platform from which Mussolini was to address an audience revealed the tracings of the stresses generated at the two massive trusses that were to support the cantilevered wall.[21] What is referred to here as a wall appears to be actually a curved

FIG 15 Giuseppe Terragni, Palazzo Littorio, Scheme A elevation, 1934

15 According to both the Zanichelli monograph and Manfredo Tafuri's *Modern Architecture,* Terragni's collaborators include A. Carminati, E. Saliva, L. Vietti, M. Nizzoli, and M. Sironi.
16 Manfredo Tafuri, "Giuseppe Terragni: Subject and Mask," trans. Diane Ghirardo, *Oppositions* (Winter 1977): 1–25.
17 "Somehow those isostatic lines explain the form of the vertical incision, marking a weak point in the curved structure; nonetheless the reason for them is still not entirely clear." Tafuri, "Giuseppe Terragni," 6.
18 R. C. Dove and Paul H. Adams, *Experimental Stress Analysis and Motion Measurement* (Columbus, OH: Charles E. Merrill, 1964), 288.
19 The question of photo-elasticity is here bound up with issues of photography and to some extent a broader interest in overexposure or the overexposing of film. Moholy Nagy's film *Light-Space Modulator* (1930) is marked by an overexposing that results at times in a blank white screen. More recently, the photography of many of Bernard Tschumi's architectural

models seems to present his buildings in some form of optic dissolve and at times blankness.
20 R. C. Dove and Paul H. Adams, *Experimental Stress Analysis,* 288.
21 Thomas Schumacher, *Surface and Symbol: Giuseppe Terragni and the Architecture of Italian Rationalism* (New York: Princeton Architectural Press, 1991), 183.
22 Schumacher, *Surface and Symbol,* 183.

diaphragm structure that operates as a thin-walled beam: in the perspective drawing that depicts the structure from above and in plan, two wall surfaces seem to compose a structure that synthetically acts as a hollow beam. As such, the suspension of this conflation of curved structural plate and box beam would have behaved very differently under loading than a single plate or wall surface would have. It is not clear if the photo-elastic analysis was performed using a diaphragm model that accurately depicted the complexity of the proposed cantilever, nor is it clear if the modeled surface employed in analysis conformed to the curvature of the actual building design. In either case, neglecting these attributes would have rendered the test results inaccurate and the resulting construction almost invariably catastrophic.

The trusses that were to support a significant portion of this surface's weight, seen in the perspective illustration from above, would not have been visible to a viewer at ground level.[22] Their support of the eighty-meter-long porphyry wall occurred at two points that straddled the removed section of construction cut out to accommodate the balcony. The cutout section effectively creates two almost independent surfaces that reconnect under the balcony; each in effect is supported at one point, but their joining also causes them to act as continuous structure. This places a great strain on the surfaces that surround the cutout. Given the slight curvature of the suspended wall surface, the pointal support of the trusses would have instigated rotational moments in not one but two axes, and each of these moments would threaten the ability of the structure to achieve or maintain equilibrium. The first rotational moment would have been parallel to the surface of the composition, and it would have induced a membraned stress across the surface of the wall; the second rotational moment would have been instigated by the slight curvature of the wall surface and its axis would have been perpendicular to this surface. Both rotations would have critically altered the degree to which the photo-elastic analysis, if performed on a flat surface, could predict the behavior of these surfaces and their beam configurations under loading. If the construction was indeed that of a thin-walled beam, how and when it would fail would be very different from that of a singular plane. The design of the building, however, appears to anticipate the complexity of forces at play and it seems intuitively to induce and counteract them. The diaphragm construction of the building's facade appears to be intended to provide the depth needed to counter these oblique loading conditions. While the shallow curvature of the plan exacerbated the capabilities of the cantilevered composition to maintain equilibrium, it also appears to provide the structural depth and ballast required to resist buckling and structural failure. The potential that the wall surface would buckle under its own loading would have been more complex at the central balcony, where a section of wall is removed. Terragni and Lingeri seemed willing to allow for both structural depth and curvature, and the concurrent deep pictorial depth and frontality that abetted the project's political requirements, while effectively trying to maintain a primarily surface or shallow distribution of stresses along the surface. The result is a construction that has qualities of both depth and surface, yet it is a composition that refuses the hierarchical dimension of either axial vector. This lack of hierarchy has confounded succinct readings of Terragni's political resolve.

If a slight adjustment were made in the calibration of surface curvature to wall thickness, wall height, vertical support, or material chemical stability, it is clear that the project could

suffer a dramatic structural collapse. Terragni and Lingeri appear to have set the project on the verge of material and formal failure: in other words, it seems that they have found a combination of formal and material properties that reveals a threat to the stability of the status quo while allowing for its ultimate and highly dramatic sustenance. In this light the complexity of Terragni's political beliefs might find some clarity. Perhaps more significant, this project reveals the status of the dialectical imperatives that define its plastic and mechanical prerogatives, and so provides a critique of its own means and those of its patronage. This is something that contemporary conscriptions of the visual do not seem to provide. The polarization of the light source in the testing process delimits the plane about which the light waves vibrate, and relies upon the discretization of axial dimensions that were otherwise potentially infinite. Understood within the cultural and political regime for which this project was designed, this delimiting of mechanical and physical cycles allows for the dialectical confinement of what would have been infinite within nature. In essence, this delimiting is the architecture of Palazzo Littorio: an artificial contrivance and model of nature's duration, a frontalized and at least partially classicized architectural design whose structural mechanics instigate a pseudo-migratory set of forces that mimic the duration of organic life. Within the discrete basin of modern engineering techniques, this dialectical device becomes a mechanical and translational model of what Guy Debord refers to as the "social appropriation of time." It is an edifice that both conceals and reveals "the power that built itself up on the basis of the penury of the society of cyclical time." Palazzo Littorio is "the power . . . of the class which organized social labor" and confiscated "the limited surplus value to be extracted" from it.[23] The Palazzo Littorio is a model of temporal surplus as disequilibrium. The surfaces upon which this power is inscribed instigate and resolve their own structural instabilities; while the relation of forces in the two cantilevers is binary, the origin of the instability appears to be migratory and floating. The resultant equilibrium is one that feigns surplus in a perpetual motion. Within the quantitative techniques of finite element analysis and the discretization of structural mechanics and optic properties of light, Terragni and Lingeri have assembled a model of structural immanence—a model that succeeds the dialectics of its own contrivance. Surely equilibrium is the necessary final state, but in choosing to represent the residual and latent forces—the surplus energies—at work in the creation of this spectacle, Terragni and Lingeri have created a critique of metropolitan dialectics and metropolitan subjectivity. This wall, an expansive painting of sorts, delivers to Mussolini the pictorial gaze of an audience whose subjectivity it both conscripts and ironically also may sever.[24] In transforming the perspectival depth of a viewing subject into the thermodynamic modeling of light as material strain within photography, Terragni and Lingeri have effectively flattened the menacing distance that segregates subject and object. In other words, it is possible to read this pictorial field as both expanded and tragically foreclosed.

In his essay "Scopic Regimes of Modernity," Martin Jay describes the distinction between "artificial" and "synthetic perspective": artificial perspective holds a flat and planar mirror up to nature and therefore produces a flattened representation; synthetic perspective employs a concave mirror and, even though the concave surface still produces an ultimately homoge-

FIG 16 Hans Hofmann, *Ecstasy*, 1947
FIG 17 Hans Hofmann, *Yellow Table on Yellow Background*, 1936

23 Guy Debord, *The Society of the Spectacle* (New York: Zone Books, 1994), 94.
24 Jonathan Crary writes in his essay "Modernizing Vision" that "the camera obscura defined an observer who was subjected to an inflexible set of positions and divisions." Crary's observer "is a nominally free sovereign individual" standing in a "quasidomestic space separated from a public exterior world." Jonathan Crary, "Modernizing Vision," in Foster, *Vision and Visuality*, ed. Hal Foster (Seattle: Bay Press, 1988), 30–32.

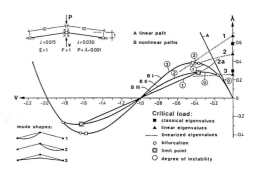

FIG 18 Critical linear and nonlinear conditions of stability in an analysis of structural mechanics

25 Martin Jay, "Scopic Regimes of Modernity," in Foster, *Vision and Visuality*, 10–11.
26 Jay, "Scopic Regimes of Modernity," 10.
27 Tafuri considered the curvature of the surface too shallow to effectively hold the space of the piazza.
28 Today this type of stress analysis is accomplished using computer modeling software and, as such, interacts differently with the eye's role in cognition.
29 A number of Terragni's projects appear to operate as thin-walled beams. The Novocomum in particular seems to operate as massive shell structure; its windows remove material in a way that causes the building's shell to take on the properties of a box beam.
30 I refer to an assortment of situations that extend from the Greek manipulation of the stylobate to correct optic curvature to the architecture of the 1984 Los Angeles Olympics, which was designed to interact with and anticipate the television camera.

neous representation of nature, it provides a multiplicity of potential vantage points.[25] The concave surface adds attributes of the infinite to the finite in its dissolution of the single station point. Synthetic perspective allows work to be "successfully viewed from more than the imagined apex of the beholder's visual pyramid."[26] The facade of Palazzo Littorio, literally a concave surface that was to embrace a delivered and frontal audience,[27] in this light espouses the homogeneity of Cartesian perspective, yet could also be said to model the autonomy of the individual within a spectacle of synthetic perspective. While such a suggestion is plausible given Terragni's affiliations with the Fascist Party, any attempt in design to transpose Terragni's mechanics to contemporary sites within contemporary regimes is haunted by an unresolved doubt. Jay clarifies this doubt in a reference to the camera obscura and the "gleeful conclusion" by Friedrich Nietzsche that "if everyone had his or her own camera obscura with a distinctly different peephole…then no transcendental world view would be possible." The monocularity of both the process by which Terragni and Lingeri attempted to deliver an audience to Mussolini and by which they employed the processes of photo-elastic analysis relied upon the discretization of vision within an evolved photographic process, a single peephole in effect, that mimicked the quantitative and monocular geometries of Cartesian perspective. The photo-elastic process could even be said to have transformed attributes of visuality into the chemical process of photography itself: the photographic surface is the hegemonic confiscation and dissolution of human vision—vision and figuration here become thermodynamic in a chemically "expanded" field. Is the curvature of Palazzo Littorio's facade a form of synthetic perspective, and if so, was Terragni interested in providing an individual and transcendent worldview? If this is a correct reading of Terragni's intentions, does this "synthetic" subjectivity provide the transcendent omniscience of its party's patronage in a monolithic form as it also provides the individuality of the single person? Given the ultimate homogeneity of synthetic perspective's structure and its ultimate failure to provide a truly unlimited number of vantage points or to relinquish enframing itself, is Palazzo Littorio an intimation of the impossibility of both transcendence and the monolithic?

The chemistry and optical mechanics of the photo-elastic processes were perfected during the 1930s as Terragni and Lingeri completed the design of their project.[28] The implementation of this experimental technique in the design of Palazzo Littorio appears to be an isolated incident employed only once in Terragni's career. Terragni did, however, design and build other projects in which this technique would have been useful, if not necessary.[29] The manner in which and for whom the Palazzo Littorio project was produced is in this sense a unique instance in the history of architecture and optical experimentation.[30] The scion of Palazzo Littorio's patronage is undeniable; the photographic and lens techniques employed in the building's design at the very least aggressively attempted a re-situating of an optic subject within a delivered mass audience. The paradigms of Cartesian perspectivalism, the monocular of camera and lens mechanics, the discovery and manipulation of light waves, and the thermodynamics of the photographic process are employed in the design of Palazzo Littorio in a way that marks this project as one of the most advanced and complex attempts in the history of architecture to inculcate space and political authority.

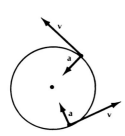
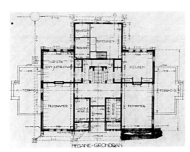

In the case of Palazzo Littorio, it is clear that Mussolini becomes the metaphoric force that prevents both the collapse of the party and, figuratively, the collapse of the architectural apparatus itself. Thomas Schumacher speculates that Terragni's lacing of porphyry, an Egyptian stone only available from a single quarry, with steel was an appropriate image for the omnipotence of Fascist ambitions. It is hard to argue with this thematically, but Terragni's recurring willingness to retain an extravagant degree of both the figural and symbolic, and his willingness to almost allow the represented within the severity of his abstracting techniques require that we speculate further about the significance of this work in a context beyond those of either state ambitions or an architect's symbolization of those ambitions.

The mechanical and translational techniques that Terragni employed in his incantation of Mussolini's authority were also employed by Terragni in different programs toward completely other ends. The seeming portability of these techniques gives validity to a strictly formal analysis, even given the circumstances of this architect's patrons. While it could be argued that all of Terragni's works were completed within the margins of Fascism, it is difficult not to see these spatial interests as perhaps more endemic to Terragni himself. It is difficult to evaluate fully the pictorial mechanics of Terragni and Lingeri's collaborative works; these projects offer an architecture of dialectic pictorial means that expresses the omniscience of authority, but also the negation of its discrete means. On a contemporary site, however, the techniques by which these projects orchestrate space offer in the catastrophe of their ocular engagement an ironic and unexpected experience. The widening of the visual field and over-dilating of the eye afford access to a mode of time as duration. As such, these techniques have value in the comprehension of the dissolute spaces of the late American metropolis.

The Centripetal and the Centrifugal: Dutch Matter

Peter Eisenman's research and analysis of Terragni's Casa Giuliani-Frigerio, published in the essay "From Object to Relationship II" more than twenty five-years ago, offer a model of Terragni's plastic mechanics that has yet to be fully assimilated into a larger critique of Terragni's enduring relevance. Casa Giuliani-Frigerio was completed in 1940, and in many ways the attributes that Eisenman reveals in this building indicate a conception of space that Terragni could not have imagined within the visual dialectics of either Palazzo Littorio's structure or Casa Rustici's perspectivalism. Only by passing through these stages and by detaching the visual from the formal could Terragni conceive of space in the manner that Eisenman presents. According to Eisenman, Casa Giuliani-Frigerio is involved in the simultaneous development of two types of space: the first considers space as subtractive, or cut away from a solid; the second considers space as additive "and understood to operate in the layering of planes." The key to Eisenman's explication is that these two techniques not only operate simultaneously, but this simultaneity reveals an ambiguity in how the project exists "plastically." Eisenman's analysis portrays a "conceptual ambiguity" developed "from the use of two opposing conceptions of space"—the centripetal subtracting of space from an existing volume or mass, and the centrifugal layering of planes in a cumulative and additive process. The analysis seeks to reveal the potential of "abstract relationships" as conceivably independent of actual ones, and proposes that the search

FIG 19 Centripetal and centrifugal acceleration: position and velocity vectors for a particle in uniform circular motion

FIGS 20–22 J. J. P. Oud, De Vonk Holiday Residence, 1919

31 Gilles Deleuze describes a scenario of two fluxes contained within a third and quotes Henri Bergson: "Such is our first idea of simultaneity. We call simultaneous, then two external fluxes that occupy the same duration because they hold each other in the duration of the third, our own simultaneity of fluxes that brings us back to internal duration, to real duration." Gilles Deleuze, *Bergsonism* (New York: Zone Books, 1988), 80.

32 Though House X was the product of a process of decomposition, the project has plastic attributes that vividly relate it to Eisenman's work on Terragni. In the design of House X, the decomposition procedures appear to give rise to an ambiguous hierarchy of centripetal and centrifugal tendencies. The grids that characterize much of the project appear at times to be recessive as well as projective, as do the building masses themselves. The project's spatial characteristics are largely those that Eisenman explicated in Terragni's Casa Giuliani-Frigerio. Eisenman's procedures also have a direct relation to Slutzky's: Eisenman presents the vertebrate structure of House VI as the result of a transformation process that bisected two initial planes and then "turned them inside out." Peter Eisenman, *House X* (New York: Rizzoli, 1982), 88. **33** Debord, *The Society of the Spectacle,* 124.

for an architectural syntax is likely to be found in the ambiguity between these conceptual and actual relationships. Eisenman's analysis ultimately tends toward a resolution of the questions of transformation and hermeneutics that preoccupy his own practice of architecture, but they might also be understood to reveal Terragni's architecture as a kind of Bergsonian duration, a type of third form that encapsulates the expansion and contraction of two types of space.[31] This offers a nonrepresentational and non-dialectic conception of matter, a conception of space that I would argue is the conception of "autonomy" that Eisenman's House X sought.[32] In his analysis of Terragni's Casa Giuliani-Frigerio, Eisenman moves the subject's cognition from the relative and the represented to the intuited and the conceptual, and in doing so places both the subject and the object within a third duration that allows the autonomy of each participant. While Casa Giuliani-Frigerio makes use of techniques endemic to pictorial space, such as frontality and depth, it does so in a multivalent manner that offers no real hierarchical viewpoint. It is perhaps the closest Terragni ever came to eradicating the vestige of perspectivalism from his work. Even if we set Terragni aside, Eisenman's interpretation of space in this manner offers a mode of spatial comprehension in its own right. Eisenman has often stated that he invented Terragni, meaning that his readings of Terragni were driven by his own concerns; given this context, it seems that Eisenman's findings are and should be transpositional—we should be able to use them in other contexts or within other regimes.

Eisenman's analysis has been criticized for isolating the formal aspects of Terragni's architecture both from the political milieu in which the works were generated and from the theological complexity of Terragni's own Catholicism. Eisenman has resisted this criticism, and in some ways this is unfortunate because the revelations of his analysis can be understood as a mechanism of a broader critique of subjectivity as it is drawn within the machinic authority of metropolitan processes. The dialectic relationship of centrifugal and centripetal forces that Eisenman's analysis disables is, in scenarios of contemporary urbanism, manifest almost exclusively by the demands of speculative capital. To quote Guy Debord, the "dictatorship of the automobile, the pilot product of the first stage of commodity abundance, has left its mark on the landscape in the dominance of freeways that bypass the old urban centers and promote even greater dispersal." The centrifugal satellite developments of Debord's scenario are themselves "subject to the irresistible centrifugal trend, and when, as partial reconstructions of the city, they in turn become overtaxed secondary centers, they are likewise cast aside." Within the machinations of a self-sustaining consumptive economy, the dissolution of the city is inevitable.[33] Eisenman's model of an ambiguous hierarchy of centripetal and centrifugal tendencies could be understood in this light to offer the possibility of an objective yet nonplastic architectural engagement in this dissolution: it seems that Eisenman found in the Casa Giuliani-Frigerio a kind of nonplastic space, a mode of willful yet nonsubjective composition, a manner of building that refuses to participate in the deployment of authority. Eisenman and Tafuri situate the bulk of their theses within the mechanisms of language; it could be argued that in doing so they suppress the potential plastic attributes of the work they analyze but also suppress its usefulness in fabricating a conception of plasticity in contemporary architectural and urban space.

Eisenman's analysis of Terragni must be understood as related to attributes of de Stijl conceptions of the real. Theo Van Doesberg wrote that "intrinsic reality" was "dynamic movement" and that this movement was established in "abstract art by the exact determination of the structure of form and space."[34] The trajectory of Terragni's experimentation as it moved from Casa Rustici and Palazzo Littorio to Casa Giuliani-Frigerio involved a search for the real as well, though this search tended to posit the real as something that must be intuited. Terragni never fully relinquished the enframing device, but he progressively diminished its presence while retaining its critical potential.

Addendum: de Stijl and the City

The question of an expansion and contraction of the visual field originated in a statement by Theo Van Doesberg about the nature of the terms "centrifugal" and "centripetal." Van Doesberg at times failed to mention the centripetal force in his descriptions of de Stijl architecture. The centripetal force is the necessary origin of the so-called centrifugal force, which in reality is not a force at all, but the inertia of an object and its tendency to move in a straight rather than curved path. This research is presented here as an addendum. I should also note that the buildings of Terragni and Lingeri inspired the use of Slutzky and Ockman's, Bryson's, and Stella's critiques. Most of the above was refined and clarified in a series of fourteen architectural projects that I designed between 1986 and 1996. Some of these thoughts were recorded in an earlier paper and project titled "House Inside Out: Unloading the Neoplastic Frame." The following section provides the context for the research attributes of the two design projects presented on these pages.

In referring to the architecture of the de Stijl movement in the essay "Sixteen Points of a Plastic Architecture," Theo Van Doesberg proclaimed that the "new architecture" was to be centrifugal in massing—"it throws its volumes from a center pinion."[35] At first glance, Van Doesberg's statement seems essentially clear, and a collection of presumed centrifugal works of architecture, from Wright to Mies to Neutra, comes to mind: the Usonian Houses, the Brick Country House, and the Kaufman Desert House are all derivations of some "pinwheel" centrifugal planning paradigm. Mies's project, however, is ambiguous in this regard—or at least its famous plan drawing is. The walls of Mies's composition, drawn in charcoal, continue to the edges of the paper—it is not clear if the generative origin of Mies's plan originates at the center of the drawing's surface or at the periphery, nor is it clear how one should view the plastic qualities of the wall masses themselves if neither tendency predominates. Historically Mies's plan is considered to have an antecedent in Van Doesberg's painting *Rhythm of a Russian Dance,* and a closer scrutiny of Van Doesberg's proclamation reveals that perhaps the architect and painter has erred in his classical—that is, physical—use of the word centrifugal. Van Doesberg has at least taken the word out of its expected context and, it seems, mistakenly severed it from its correlative and originating relation to a centripetal force. Mies, Wright, and Neutra aside, what follows is an attempt to clarify the potential of Van Doesberg's possible misuse of the word centrifugal as well as to speculate on the implications of what seems to be Van Doesberg's fortuitous lack of research into the analogy he has drawn from physics. Van Doesberg's mistaken use of the word centrifugal may have been

34 Hans Ludwig C. Jaffé, *De Stijl 1917–1931: The Dutch Contribution to Modern Art* (Cambridge, MA, and London: Belknap Press, 1986), 109.

35 "The new architecture is anti-cubic, that is to say, it does not try to freeze the different functional space cells in one closed cube. Rather, it throws the functional space cells (as well as the overhanging planes, balcony volumes, etc.) centrifugally from the core of the cube. And through this means, height, width, depth, and time (i.e., an imaginary but four-dimensional entity) approaches a totally new plastic expression in open spaces. In this way architecture acquires a more or less floating aspect that, so to speak, works against the gravitational forces of nature." Theo Van Doesberg, "Sixteen Points of a Plastic Architecture," in Kenneth Frampton, *Modern Architecture: A Critical History* (London: Thames and Hudson, 1980), 145.

intended and if it was, the spatial implications of this use reveal a complexity in the spatial ideals not only of de Stijl architecture but also, if extrapolated, of contemporary sites or the white rectangle of contemporary cities.

A centrifugal force is a reactive force, and in the strictest sense of the word it is actually not a force at all. What we call a centrifugal force is actually the inertia of an object as it tries to move along a straight path while being held in a circular one by a correlative centripetal force. Physicists refer to a centripetal force as center-seeking—it is the force that holds an object in a circular motion. A centrifugal force is referred to as center-fleeing, but in actuality this is not a force per se. What we call a centrifugal force arises within the object's attempt to move along a straight path tangential to the circular acceleration of the object's movement. The magnitude of a centrifugal force is defined by the inertia of the object, by its tendency to stay in motion. One then wonders whether Van Doesberg was loosely using a metaphor drawn from another field of inquiry, or whether he actually meant that the spatial qualities of de Stijl architecture were defined outside this otherwise dialectical relationship of opposing "forces." It seems that the latter is closer to the truth because Van Doesberg's statement, in its continuity, refers to a plastic ideal that ultimately is ambiguous in its spatial character. In Van Doesberg's proclamation, the new architecture was to have "a more or less floating aspect," an aspect that "works against the gravitational forces of nature." If the reactive tendencies of centrifugal and centripetal forces were somehow loosened or alleviated in the above physical model, something close to this effect would be achieved. The canonical de Stijl architectural compositions of Van Doesberg and Van Eesteren were supposed to be read as "more or less floating" and ultimately as neither centripetal nor centrifugal. In his omission of the term centripetal was Van Doesberg trying to describe a centrifugal plastic quality unanchored by an opposing centripetal force—a centrifugal "force" without an originary point? If this is the case, the idealized plastic qualities of a de Stijl composition are to be understood as existing outside the dialectics of the opposing forces of centripetal and centrifugal, but how can such a composition cohere? How do we characterize the forces that assure its compositional density yet do not operate in a dialectical manner? Depending on where one looks within the de Stijl oeuvre and to which practitioner one turns, vastly different ways of answering these questions arise.

Mondrian, for example, spoke of composition in the form of both "static balance" and "dynamic equilibrium." In this paradigm, static balance defined the unity of individual forms within a composition, while dynamic equilibrium unified these individual elements in opposition. In this context, Van Doesberg is perhaps again errant in his description of physical laws, but his intention is nonetheless clear and could be situated within the problem as stated by Mondrian. To the static balance of individual forms Mondrian applied the term "limitation"; I would apply centripetal. To the term dynamic equilibrium Mondrian attached the term "extension"; I would apply centrifugal. But Mondrian goes further and gives insight into Van Doesberg's use of centrifugal in other dimensions: "Ultimately dynamic equilibrium destroys static balance."[36] It seems possible to understand Van Doesberg's intentions in this context: the extension of a centrifugal force would destroy the delimiting centripetal force that defined both the static balance of the individual components and the static balance of the complete composition itself. If Van Doesberg could alleviate the centripetal force—or at least its originary qualities—in defining the plasticity of his composition yet still not relinquish the vitalizing qualities of centrifugal extension, he could ascribe to these compositions a state of independence, autonomy, and self-description that was neither entropic nor metaphysical. Van Doesberg's architectural masterworks were confined to his projects with Van Eesteren, and they were to a great extent not constructed. Practice would surely have challenged the "more or less floating" aspect of these compositions.

In his De Vonk Holiday Residence (1919), J. J. P. Oud seems to have masterfully incorporated the bulk of Van Doesberg's polemic and the added dimension of gravity as it defines weight and mass. Here Oud mastered not only the simultaneous dynamics of the centrifugal and the centripetal, but also added the tectonics and weight of material to the equation—something Van Doesberg's drawings were not required to reconcile. This is a building that seems to be at once additive and centrifugal in massing, yet subtractive and centripetal in volume. The masonry wall appears to be conceived of as hollowed out from inside—cored down to the severe thinness that reveals the tenuous stability of stacking bricks in a planar formation. Yet the building itself is also expansive in an admittedly tempered but de Stijl massing of its primary blocks. Oud's walls seem dangerously thin, and it is clear that the architect was interested in hewing them to a planar quality. The stair of the De Vonk residence sets in motion a complex reading of central and peripheral spatial mechanisms that further complicate this planar expansion of volume. The stair is flanked by two columns that carry the weight of the second floor above; these columns instigate a sense of weight that the stair seems to contravene as it tosses itself up through the opening in the floor. The stair seems to turn the space of the residence inside out—it is a topological device, a kind of horizontal oculus that threatens a rearrangement of the centripetal and centrifugal characteristics of the building's spaces. Oud, always a reluctant comrade of Van Doesberg, managed a feat of neoplastic space within the constraints of actual gravity and constituent material weight.

Though I do not believe the preceding assertions are something to prove or disprove critically, the omniscience and inevitability of dialectics in reference to the definition of a plastic work of art or architecture are revealed to be less conclusive than assumed. The questions are interesting to follow because they are rooted in the mechanics of physics, and to some degree it is possible to quantify our speculations. These questions are most interesting as they lead historically across a trajectory of architectures and architects of vastly different social and political situations. Frank Gehry's Hollywood Public Library would lend itself to this type of analysis. Peter Eisenman has spent a large part of his career looking for the mode of analysis that could reveal or produce this nondialectical ambiguity and one could argue that in fact he has achieved this if his work is viewed as a kind of Debord surplus—if we read the hermetic mechanics of its presumed autonomy as providing the surface upon which power may either be individually inscribed or withheld from politically fascist assertion. As such, architecture succeeds in what it manages to keep at bay. Given the degree to which the contemporary site of architecture is constructed by the invisible and the predatory, this should be a note of ironic strength. A Cartesian and almost nondialectical form of space and architecture could be understood ironically to provide a resistive critique

FIG 23 Satellites and cars—preparing the infrastructural topologies of the megalopolis: Naval Research Labs electronics engineer William Bell supervises the loading of a communications satellite payload into a rented Ford Galaxy 500 at White Sands, New Mexico, 1968

of the dynamically mobile and exponentially trabeated orchestrations of labor and material in all modes of contemporary life. This form also provides both a critique of subjugation and a resourcing and aesthetic rejection of easily fabricated standard tectonic means. We shall live upon the inside-out surface of produced space.

"HAVING HEARD MATHEMATICS: The Topologies of Boxing" first appeared in *Slow Space*, edited by Michael Bell and Sze Tsung Leong.

Duration House

Client Ruston Alsbrooks **Site** Houston, Texas
Date of Design 1995–97 **Status** Designed **Budget** $200,000

In the post-1980s oil bust, Houston's economy, inextricably linked to world oil production, collapsed, and block after block of buildings in what is known as midtown—an area that stretches from the city's apparent downtown to the museum district, Rice University, and Hermann Park—were left empty. By the mid-1990s, midtown began to flourish again as it was redeveloped with housing, although today it still has a large number of vacant lots. These three buildings and courtyards—comprising a house, an office, and a greenhouse—collect a series of those empty spaces to form a compound on a corner site in this area.

The structure was designed for a Houston police officer who initially wanted to replicate a modern house from the city's River Oaks residential section. The topology of holes in midtown, however, instigated the design of a house that was largely vacant: three courtyards became its predominant features. The construction is simple tilt-up concrete and steel-frame window walls. The house is modest in size and materials, but the spaces recall the urbanism of Houston's boom and bust; they seek a tempered sense of the city's emptiness. The Duration House won a *Progressive Architecture* design award in 1996. It was one of fourteen projects awarded out of 444 international entries. It was also the central work in the 1996 exhibition "Endspace: Michael Bell and Hans Hofmann" at the Berkeley Art Museum, organized by Lawrence Rinder (now a curator at the Whitney Museum of American Art in New York).

"The visible is only the final step of an historic form. Its true fulfillment. Then it breaks off and a new world arises."
—Mies van der Rohe

Views Toward Downtown

This photo was taken on San Jacinto Street, just south of site. Wood-frame houses are still predominant on some blocks despite the proximity of new development.

Space in the megalopolis has lost its elastic strength. Atrophied and limp, it no longer provides plazas on boulevards to shore up its occupants. A cross-country excursion from Houston to San Francisco is startling and numbing at the same time: In San Antonio, Fort Stockton, El Paso, Tucson, Phoenix, San Bernardino, Pomona, Fresno, and San Jose, the proliferation of economic types continues—Wal-Marts, Office Depots, and car dealerships have outpaced virtually all city forms. There are no new streets (even New Urbanist streets aren't really streets), only parking lots and feeder roads. The automobile has been the dominant urban catalyst for the past sixty years.

The space of the contemporary megalopolis is thin; the metropolis had thickness, even if was simply based on the inertia of matter and the linear growth of finance. In California and Texas, our two most populous states, the word *city* is a nostalgic term. The traditional city, dense at its core and progressively less so at its edges, is the counterpoint to the megalopolis, whose variations of density follow no direct or linear progressions. These patterns of density are perhaps primarily financial; a Wal-Mart is economically dense yet its surrounding parking lot is fearfully thin. By now it must be clear that, having lost virtually every race against the mechanic efficiency of the megalopolis, the city itself is thin; it has not been erased but has instead been left to catch up. When the traditional city isn't shored up by tax abatements, historic revival, or a sheer will to urbanism, we are left in the strange position of looking for an after-the-fact city and subject. How does this subject find itself, its edges, its centers, its ground? Unhinged and over-coded, a product of received information, our contemporary subject is looking for a city.

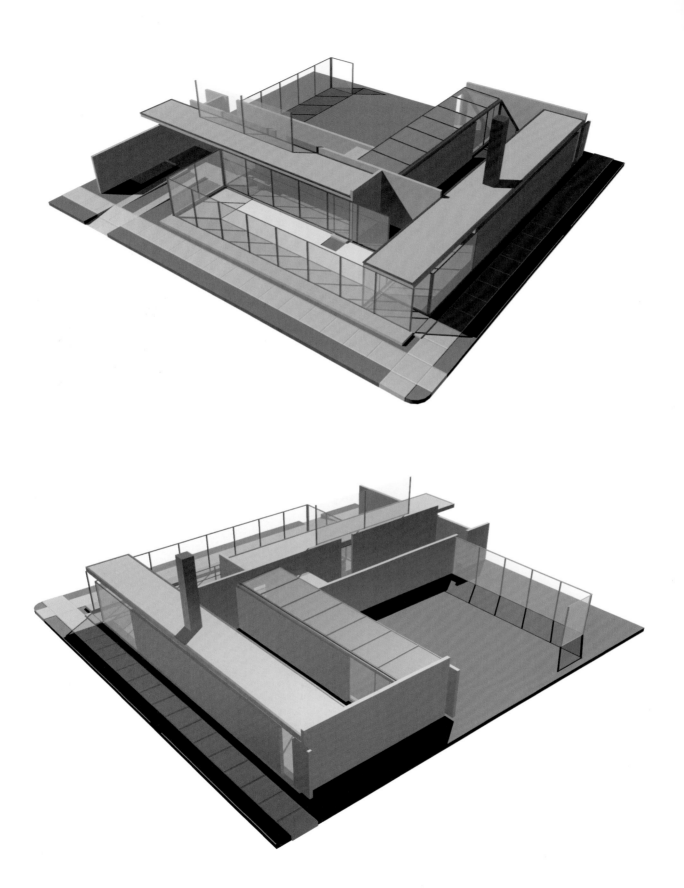

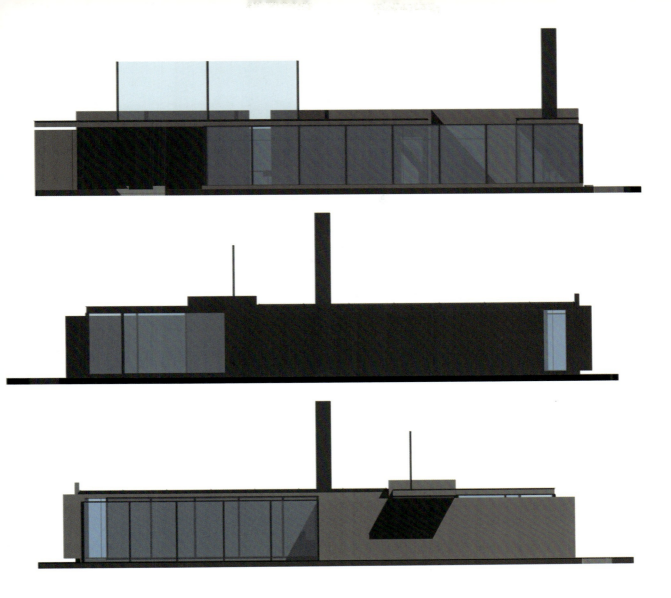

Houston Has Had Several Breaking Offs

Newcomers to this Gulf Coast metropolis can only imagine the magnitude of the oil market's collapse in the early 1980s. Oil industry jobs were lost in such numbers that houses and businesses were simply abandoned when buyers failed to materialize. Houston's massive growth trajectory of the 1970s came to a drastic halt a decade later when the form of downtown Houston—its skyscrapers and office temples—broke. The city is now so strangely surreal that it seems almost impossible to characterize it,

but the issues it raises must be taken seriously; one can only speculate about what new world can or will arise in its place.

Midtown remains dormant despite numerous redevelopment plans. In 1994, there were proposals for tax abatements, empowerment zones, and incentives that would encourage development. At the moment virtually no one lives downtown—in a metropolis of almost four million people, only a miniscule number live adjacent to the postcard skyline. While this scenario exists in other American

cities, in Houston there are open blocks next to fifty-five-story towers. Covered in the kind of vegetation that must have been there five hundred years ago, parts of Houston seem botanically ancient, and one can certainly get a sense of what the first settlers must have faced.

It is obviously a misnomer to call Houston a city; it has virtually none of the spatial or material attributes that defined the form of the traditional city. In fact, an absence of buildings is its most striking feature; the urbanist figure-ground drawing here is of no help. Houston does

have a form of material integrity derived from standardized building processes, but the question is, where one would locate the "form" of Houston—in the towers and the city grid or the economic mechanism that built them? How Houston stands up—how its buildings resist gravity and how its walls are constructed—has almost nothing to do with those traditional carriers of urban integrity: bearing, material density and quality, and human-scale enterprise.

What is the role of the architect who senses the transformed spatiality of this city

and yet is confined to the edges of a site and the traditional framework of architectural practice? In other words, what can a building do to make the city cohere in an urban condition that rabidly consumes mimicry, contextualism, and even aesthetic revolt? There are millions of cars in Houston, but almost no pedestrians, and the city's economy is more likely to be physically centered in Saudi Arabia than it is in the after-hours, peopleless downtown. What is the shape of time in a city that pulls the eye well outside the basin of vision?

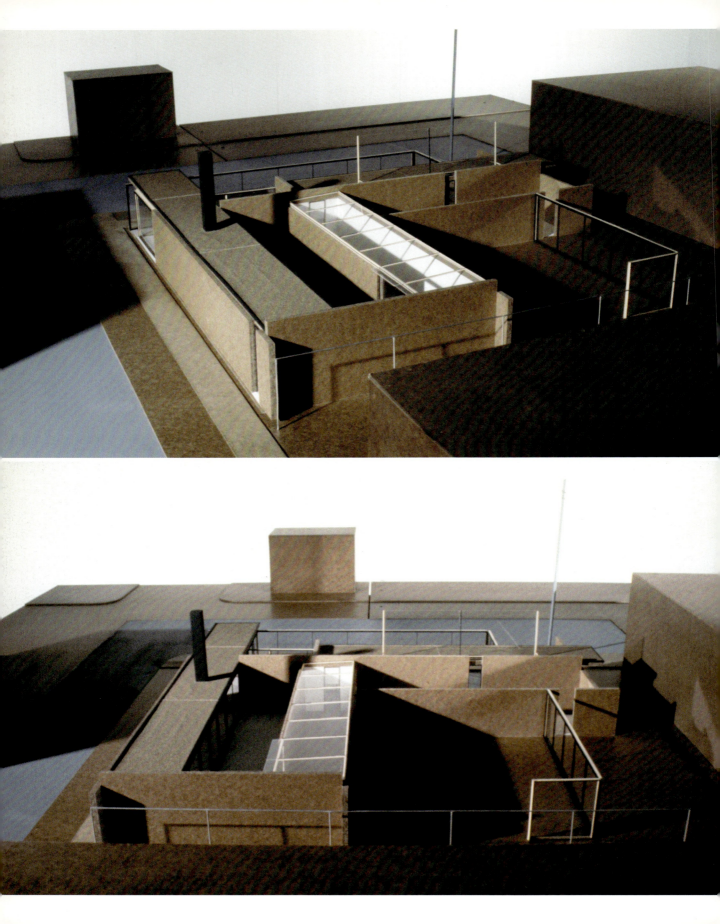

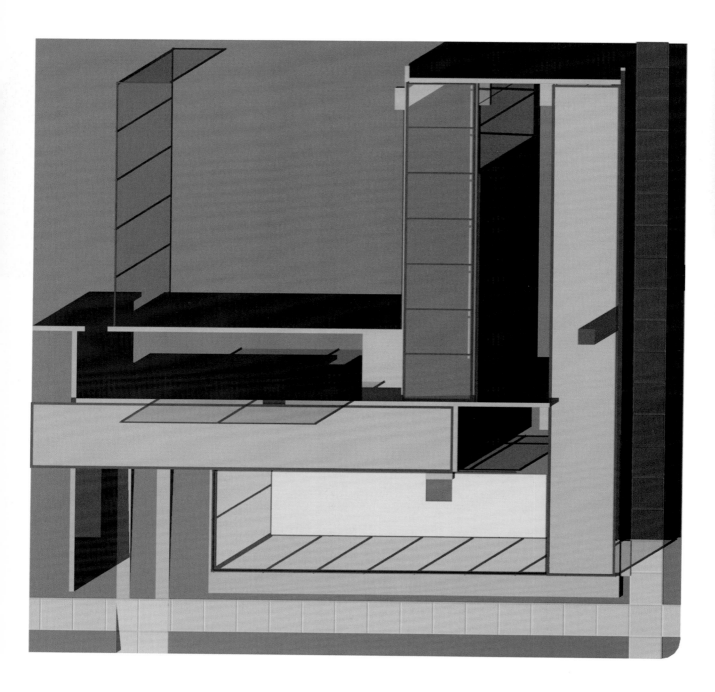

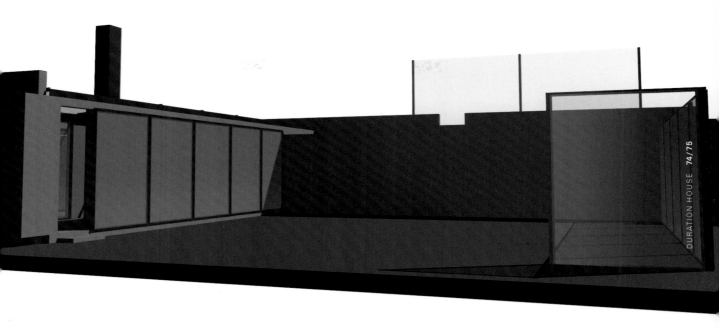

A House and Studio on the Edge of Downtown Houston

Ad Reinhardt, says Robert Smithson, is obsessed by what George Kubler called "the space between events," "the interchronic pause when nothing is happening," and "actuality." Reinhardt tries to give shape to this "interchronic" moment by developing what Smithson calls "shapes that evade shape."[1]

If market capitalism is, as Félix Guattari says, an encompassing "shape . . . a fetishized passion" of infinite dexterity that to an intolerable degree constitutes contemporary life, what "shape-evading shapes" need to be instigated in the usually finite basins of architecture?[2]

In the thin city of capital—the city we have been building for at least thirty years—architecture must administer and cohere the vacant topologies of economic and urban time.

We need shape-evading buildings that are faster than money, whose slow material duration is undetected by the market. A building that could induce fantastic topologies of matter, space, and time would provide a kind of capital-evading reflex to a modern psychasthenic subject.

1 Robert Smithson, "Quasi Infinities and the Waning of Space," in *The Writings of Robert Smithson*, ed. Nancy Holt (New York: New York University Press, 1979), 35.
2 Félix Guattari, "Regimes, Pathways, Subjects," in *Incorporations*, ed. Jonathan Crary and Sanford Kwinter (New York: Zone Books, 1992), 26.

Two Architectural Durations

Matter/Movement: held in a taxis of torsional equipoise, topologies of membrane stress migrate spontaneously through and across a rigid Cartesian basin of plate glass and flat iron.

Subjects/Movement: nomadic promenades among material durations—a nonplastic basin.

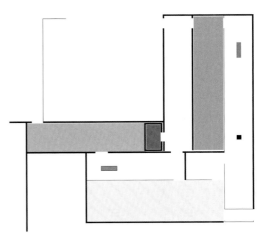

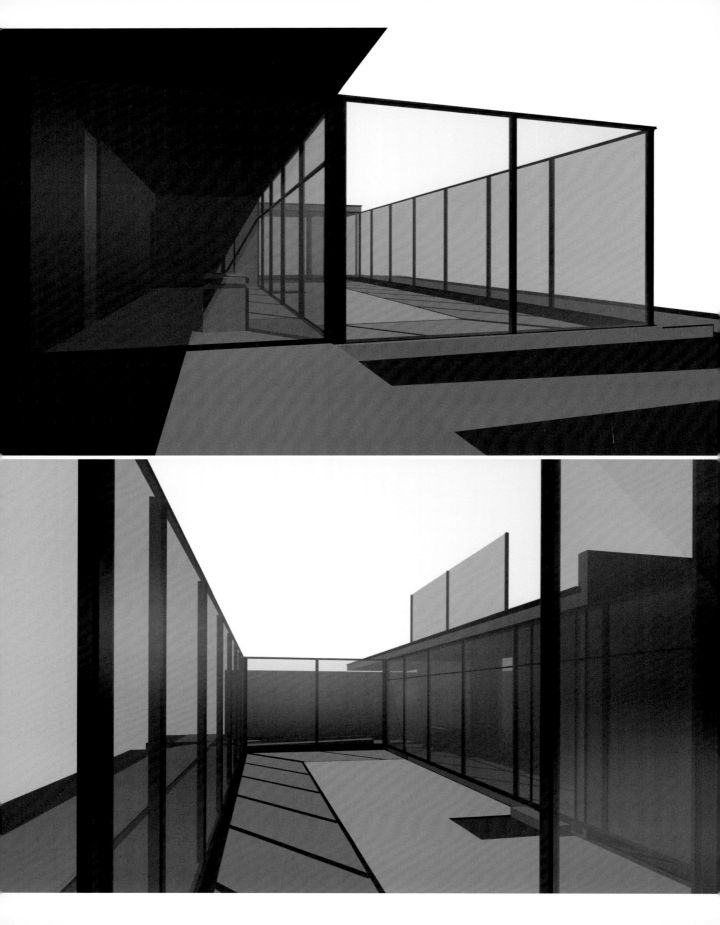

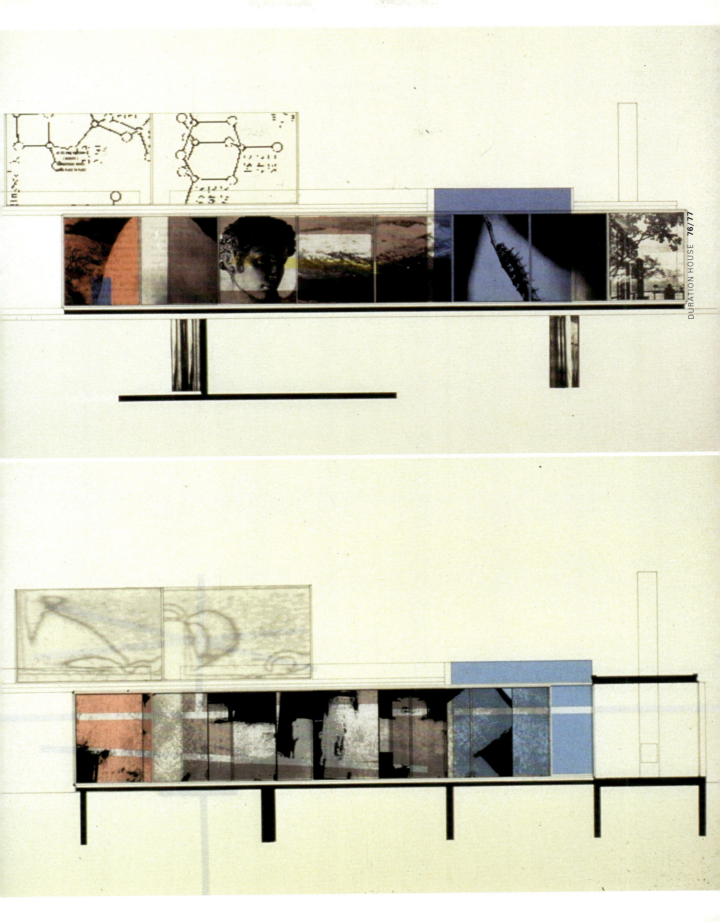

Endspace:
Michael Bell and Hans Hofmann

Client The University Art Museum, University of California, Berkeley, and Lawrence Rinder, Twentieth Century Art **Date of Design** 1995
Exhibition Dates March 15–August 20, 1995 **Budget** $26,000

An installation and exhibition at the University Art Museum in Berkeley, California, designed by Michael Bell and curated by Lawrence Rinder, the exhibition paired fourteen paintings from the museum's Hans Hofmann collection with eight architectural projects by Michael Bell.

City Inside Out

In the contemporary city, we are forced to look for what architect Albert Pope has called an "unconstructed subject." It is a scenario that differs vastly from the convulsive and total metropolitan subjugation described in Georg Simmel's 1903 essay "The Metropolis and Mental Life." In Simmel's devastating analysis, the intellect is the propellant force of the metropolis: "'The nervous life' of the metropolis therefore does not by any means lead back to 'deep regions of the personality,'" but is instead a reason for itself, he concludes. The intellect is a kind of evolutionary organ that satiates the needs of the metropolis. Our subject, on the cusp of two spaces, is both over- and under-constructed—shored up by over-coding yet dissipative in a vacant post-urban basin.

An Afterimage of the Metropolis

Tier One: Syncopation and Vision, or Space Inside Out; What If Push Didn't Answer Pull?

"Push responds to pull." Hans Hofmann used the phrase so often that it became almost universally associated with his work. The spatial milieu of a Hofmann painting is one of complex geometries cohering active and reactive forces; in Hofmann's realm, a pictorial push into space is answered by a rebounding pull back out. Of course, these pushes and pulls are achieved not with the weight of gravity but with the weights of color, shape, and line, all activated by the velocity of vision and played out within the basin of the picture's surface. Hofmann's paintings are plastic, meaning that their space is active in the way it animates the initially neutral picture surface.

Hans Hofmann's spatial trajectory seems to have moved in a staccato rhythm; innovations led to innovations, but also back to his foundations. One such foundation was his preoccupation with Matisse's particular structure of flat space. In works such as *Yellow Table on Yellow Background* (1936), Hofmann tilts space forward to such a degree that it threatens to spill out of its frame. The paint is thick and applied with an aggres-

sive stroke, but the space, if spilled, would certainly lose its thickness. *Yellow Table on Yellow Background* is a subjectless work: no human figure is present and one wonders where such a figure could be placed if it were.

The idea of an active, viscous, and thickened space also characterizes theories of architecture. Robert Slutzky's depiction of a plastic cubist space in the later works of the magnificent architect Le Corbusier portrays a fully alluvial space, the characteristics of which are best described in terms supplied by fluid mechanics. Le Corbusier's work was home to a vigorous and athletic modern occupant, with his promenade being energetic enough to push through such thick space.

But what if push didn't answer pull? What if space wasn't plastic or viscous? What if it were more of an energy sink, with a dissipative quality, its basin involved in an expansive entropic creep rather than a shoring-up contraction? Hofmann's thesis demands a rebuttal, just as Slutzky's and Le Corbusier's "thickened space" demands thinned space. That the antithesis of each argument has an asymptotic relation to the space we occupy in the modern "city" should cause alarm: space in the contemporary city of finance must surely be nonplastic; what viscous pulls shore us up and react to our pushes?

The antithesis of the stability of Hofmann's binary push-pull relationship does, in fact, appear in his own work: *Ecstasy* (1947) so fully exploits its flat canvas surface that push seems to make the picture frame's geometry implode, while pull threatens to spill its contents onto the gallery floor. The opposing forces' ability to

counter each other is lost here, as each seems to have exceeded its elastic limits: push and pull attain a new independence that threatens the works' stability when each is stretched beyond its capacity to rebound.

Turning space inside out has also been a preoccupation of Robert Slutzky's. The younger painter, one of our great architectural critics and a master of pictorial mechanics himself, must surely have studied Hofmann's oeuvre. The spatial forms so active in *Ecstasy* require the skills of a topologist for precise description. Topology is the branch of geometry that describes complex surfaces and the relationship of points along such surfaces; the Menger sponge and Mobius strip are primary topological forms. In the film *Turning a Sphere Inside Out*, the topological equation that describes such a process is depicted in stages. An initial push creates a cavity in the bottom of the sphere; a continued push causes the cavity to eventually reach the underside of the top of the sphere. An elastic threshold is then crossed, as push becomes pull and the cavity moves through the top of the sphere. As the other surfaces follow, the sphere is eventually pulled completely through itself before regaining its original platonic stability. The unstable interim stages appear remarkably similar to the painting *Ecstasy*. In that realm, push did not respond to pull. Rather, push continued and continued until it became a kind of limp pull. What type of space emerges at the resolution of such a process?

The pictorial mechanics of *Ecstasy* surely offer an alternative to the hegemony of perspective; here, as space is pulled inside out, the surface, the frame, and indeed the picture itself relinquish per-

spective's placement of its subject. In the essay "Modernizing Vision," Jonathan Crary analyzes the camera obscura as a model of modern subjectivity that "defined an observer who was subjected to an inflexible set of positions and divisions."[1] The spectacle of camera obscura required an acquiescent subject, one who knew where to stand. Crary's observer "is a nominally free sovereign individual" standing in a "quasi-domestic space separated from a public exterior world."[2]

The Double Dihedral House, the Berlin Stoa, and the Blue House all use the oculus as a device to syncopate vision and the perspectival field in a way that might spill their framed contents and alter their static basins. In these projects vision has a syncopated "pulse" that threatens the stability of ocular distance. The relationship of perceiving subject and perceived object is here turned inside out, overcoming the hegemony of perspective's constructed subject and its fixed basin.

1 Jonathan Crary, "Modernizing Vision," in *Vision and Visuality*, ed. Hal Foster (Seattle: Bay Press, 1988), 35.
2 Crary, "Modernizing Vision," 36.

Tier Two: Form, Immanence, and Time

The second grouping of architectural projects—the Physics Kindergarten and the Glass House—rearranges the geometry of push and pull: the window still operates as an oculus or lens, but instead of modulating depth, it functions as a puncture that instigates stress along the wall surface. If subversion of perspectival stability modulated the spatial activity of the first group, here the stress of gravity on matter and form activates the set of migrating forces along the building's surface. The status quo—a strong building form—is configured in a way that perpetuates an actively changing and topologically complex set of vital forces. In these projects, the building's shell, while structurally and formally finite, is the template that manifests membranous torsional forces.

These buildings are structural shells. As a shoe box has strength far greater than its material, so do these projects. Repositories of immanent time, "immobile cyclones," they are bundles of other forms and other temporalities. Hofmann, too, made space by activating forces along the surface of the canvas. *Lucidus Ordo* (1962) slides its color geometries across an imploding, spiraling abyss.

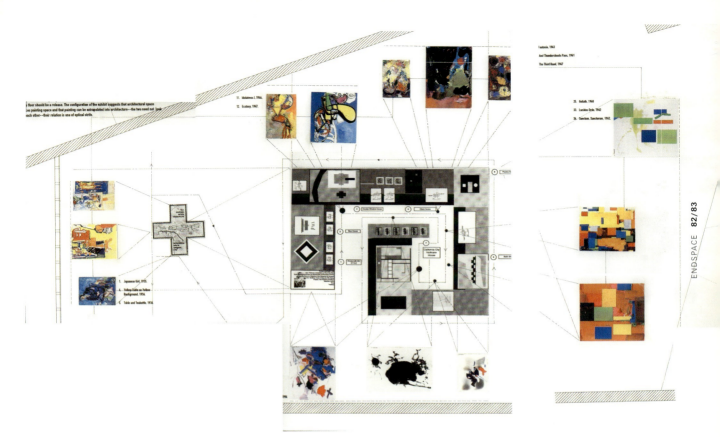

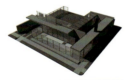

Tier Three:
Matter and Time

When a brittle material such as glass is tempered, it is reheated after formation and allowed to cool naturally; as a result, it can withstand severe perpendicular forces, but is easily fractured by a slight tap to its edge. Tempered glass is stressed along its outermost surface.

Like concrete and steel, the magnificent advances in the production of glass in the last century are the result of breakthroughs in material science and chemical engineering. What is certainly true is that material has properties of time and structure intrinsic to building form, and the third tier of projects isolates this relationship of matter and form: the way matter acts under stress and strain and, as in the case of the Houston project, specifically under shear. Here glass and concrete plates are arranged as a house of cards, reliant not merely on the structure of formal relationships, but on the structure of matter itself and the structure of time in matter.

Duration and Coherence: Passionate Economies and Slow Space—Five Chapters

1. Topology

In *The Shape of Time*, George Kubler develops a concept of duration that distinguishes between the way inorganic and organic entities exist in time. He argues that inorganic entities, in fact, do not exist in time at all, but in a kind of continuity that can't be measured in calendric, lunar, or biologic time. The sculptor Robert Smithson was deeply affected by Kubler's writing; in the essay "Quasi Infinities and the Waning of Space," he analyzes a spectrum of art, physics, and mathematics, which he relates to Kubler's description of actuality as "the space between events" and "the interchronic pause when nothing is happening," a shapeless duration.[1] Smithson tries to give shape to this interchronic, unstable, and perhaps even imperceptible

"moment"; to do so, such art has to develop shapes that evade shape.

2. Topology and Urban Economies

In an interview conducted in January of 1993, Noam Chomsky was asked if he thought America was "in for a long, painful era of unresolved economic decay." In his response, Chomsky made a distinction between the geographical United States and American corporations: the country itself, he said, was no doubt in for a period of decay—the United States, he said, was "developing characteristics of the third world"—but he speculated that its corporate share of worldwide production was probably increasing. According to Chomsky, capital generated within an evolving global economy is no longer distributed in centripetal and centrifugal patterns, or in relation to geographic origins. In places like New York, Houston, or Los

Angeles, the economic, private, and public shapes of the city have not only lost their territorial relation to an origin, but have left their inhabitants without a collective imagination of power's origin.

3. Passionate Economic Shapes

Across the spectrum of contemporary urban theory, design, and criticism one finds a recurrent theme: the inhabitant of the modern megalopolis resides within "the headlong race," "the capitalist passion that sweeps up everything in its path": "Each of their organs and social relations are quite simply re-patterned in order to be reallocated, overcoded, in accordance with the global requirements of the system."[2] The practices of architecture and urbanism appear under such conditions to be alternately temporarily recuperative and plaintive (as in New Urbanism) or opaque (to para-

phrase Rem Koolhaas: Architecture can reveal. Reveal what? The complete dominance of money.).

4. Geography: Hypersphere

Applications of Demography, The Population Situation in the U.S. in 1975 identified three dimensions of population data: the spatial, the qualitative, and the temporal.[3] According to this publication, the spatial dimension "deals with geographic distribution of people, including the density of distribution" and "the temporal dimension relates to the past, present and future of the population factors." In 2004, the question is certainly more complex. The distribution of capital that might have nourished a more or less centrifugal and dense urban geography during an industrial age is not likely to do either in the global decades. The density of the world city—its spatial and temporal dimensions—takes

on the topological geometries of the hypersphere or the Menger sponge.[4] Capital generated in a global economy will certainly be invested in the United States, but the geography of capital distribution in such an economy suggests that many American cities could easily remain fragmented and hollowed out. Cities such as Houston seem to have little chance of developing the kind of distribution of capital that could transfigure them into a traditional urban form. Conventional wisdom may be that the new global markets will change the shape of the city, but we should be prepared for the possibility that many American cities are likely to remain exactly the same.

5. Fast Buildings

Chomsky's forecast prefigures a two-tiered society— islands of wealth for investors and milieus of despair for the "restless many."[5] On what grounds

can the urban respond to such an inside-out scenario? What shape could cohere the shape-evading topology of a world city in a global economy? As Chomsky's scenario begins to play itself out, the role of creating urban coherence falls increasingly to the architect and the building. In other words, if the city is not going to cohere—if tax bases, zoning, and even public will fail to provide the centrifugal energy that might nourish traditional paradigms of urban density—then traditional urban morphology is no longer reliable. In the thin city of capital, the city we have been building for at least thirty years, it seems that buildings must take on the responsibility of administering urban time. We need either very fast or very slow buildings—buildings faster than money and markets or buildings with a slow duration the market can't access. Certainly modern painters of complex topologies are

invaluable, as are buildings that could induce the fantastic topologies of modern space, thereby providing a kind of stealth, capital-evading reflex to a modern citizen engulfed by the overspill.

1 Robert Smithson, *The Writings of Robert Smithson*, ed. Nancy Holt (New York: New York University Press, 1979).
2 Félix Guattari, "Regimes, Pathways, Subjects," in *Incorporations*, ed. Jonathan Crary and Sanford Kwinter (New York: Zone Books, 1992), 21.
3 Donald J. Boque, ed., *Applications of Demography, The Population Situation in the U.S. in 1975* (Oxford, OH: Miami University Press, 1975).
4 Ivars Peterson, *The Mathematical Tourist: Snapshots of Modern Mathematics* (New York: W. H. Freeman, 1988), 56–59.
5 David Barsamian, "The New Global Economy," in *The Prosperous Few and the Restless Many* (Berkeley: Odonian Press, 1993), 8.

Chrome House

Client Briony Gannon and James Sweet **Site** West End, Houston, Texas
Date of Design 1998–99 **Status** Designed **Budget** $186,000

This loft and photography studio for a Houston couple was designed to serve as both a residence and a place of business. The single structure also provides an office for a small graphic design studio. The building site is a typical Houston lot of fifty by a hundred feet in a part of the city known as West End, which has been under gentrification pressure as it is adjacent to River Oaks, an affluent residential neighborhood, and the Buffalo Bayou as well as downtown. It is a mixed-use area, with car repair businesses next to housing and structures that range from bungalows to prefabricated metal buildings. While these kinds of juxtapositions are typical in Houston—there is no citywide zoning—this region of the city is even more diverse and fragmented.

By using a prefabricated metal building system manufactured by Butler Buildings (which featured lightweight materials assembled with simple labor techniques), it was possible to construct more than thirty-five hundred square feet of space on a very small budget. Other low-cost items such as sliding-glass doors and aluminum window sections were also used, as were simple solar orientation techniques. The design makes a domestic space out of a building that appears industrial, and it sits comfortably in a rapidly changing neighborhood that accommodates both uses.

"Welcome to the end of the American Dream: an aluminum-clad loft has replaced home on the range," writes the critic Aaron Betsky, describing the project. "Metal shines in the Texas sun. A wall of doors opens to whatever breeze might find its way through the sprawl of Houston. Everything flows, shimmers, and shines; nothing sits still. The only thing fixing you to a place is a grid of anonymous construction. You are at once free and in limbo."

Northern Light
A garden is formed on the north side of the property; the front of the building houses a photographer's studio and the rear contains a living loft. Twelve sets of sliding-glass doors form a window wall.

A Roll-Up Metal Door Provides Access to the Studio
The entry to the living loft is on the left, and the entry to the photography studio is to the right. The second-floor window provides a view to the street and illuminates the graphic design studio.

West Surfaces

House 1 House 2 House 3 House 4 House 5 House 6

East Surfaces

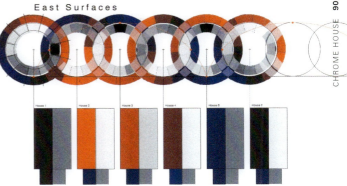

House 1 House 2 House 3 House 4 House 5 House 6

Interior Colors

Derived from a color wheel customized for various solar orientations, the warm hues face south, and the cool face north. The wheel is rotated to form a cycloid that assigns a spectrum of colors to each surface.

Window Wall

Reflecting interior and exterior color systems, the north facade registers natural phenomena and mechanical effects.

Across the Garden

The owners used processes derived from printing and mechanical reproduction techniques to create murals for the courtyard.

South Surfaces

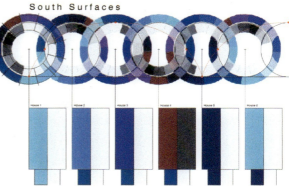

House 1 House 2 House 3 House 4 House 5 House 6

North Surfaces

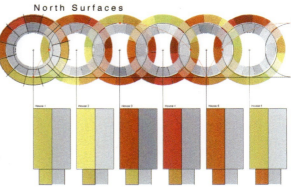

House 1 House 2 House 3 House 4 House 5 House 6

Conversation

Two steel stairs lead to the living and working lofts above the studio, which are divided by a translucent wall. A multiuse aluminum counter runs the length of the loft against the south wall, and glass and mirrored storage closets cantilevered from four-inch structural columns enclose the sleeping loft.

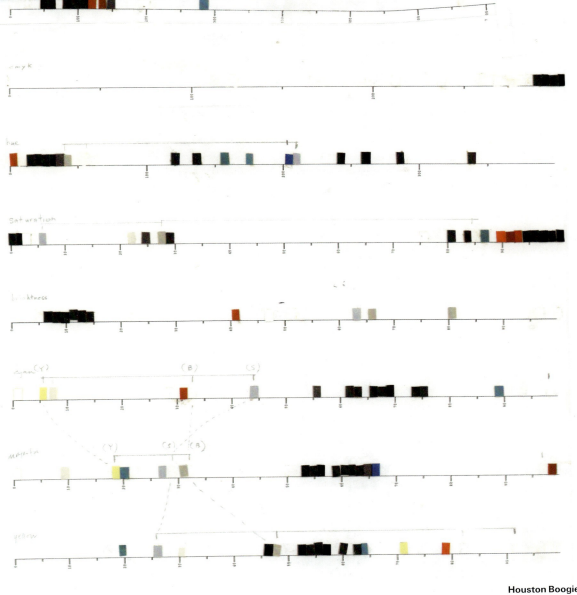

cmyk

hue

saturation

brightness

cyan (Y)   (B)   (S)

magenta   (Y)   (S) (B)

yellow

Houston Boogie Woogie
To experiment with assign-
ing colors to building surfaces, Audi A-4 colors were
analyzed for CMYK, RGB,
and HSB values. When a
particular value was chosen
as the primary organiza-
tional mode—for example,
the cyan value—it estab-
lished a unique set of linear
relations for each new
sequence; choosing cyan
afforded a very different
organization than choosing
magenta.

16 Houses:
Owning a House in the City

Client Fifth Ward Community Redevelopment Corporation
Site Fifth Ward, Houston, Texas **Date of Design** 1998 **Status** Ongoing

Part exhibition, part building program, part research project, and most important, a collective work of architecture and planning, 16 Houses developed in three distinct phases. Each stage relied on the expertise of new participants and was funded by different sources.

The project was founded in 1995 with funding from the Graham Foundation of Chicago; the first three years consisted of a study of the economics and design of the single-family house and its pivotal role in down-payment voucher programs initiated by the federal government. The primary goal was to examine the architectural implications of the new federal policy of decentralization and dispersal.

In April 1998, sixteen architects were invited to assemble teams to design single-family houses for the Fifth Ward Community Redevelopment Corporation in Houston. An exhibition of the projects, "16 Houses: Owning a House in the City," opened on November 6, 1998, at DiverseWorks in Houston. More than a thousand people crowded the gallery on opening night. Over six hundred invitations were sent to Fifth Ward residents in addition to the nine hundred people on the DiverseWorks mailing list. Two community events supported the exhibition: a midday discussion with the designers for area students and a panel discussion, held on December 12, 1998, with guests from the community. In the spring of 1999, the exhibition traveled to the University of Texas at Austin.

The third phase started in 2000, when a selection committee chose seven of the sixteen projects to be built. Funding from the Local Initiatives Support Corporation of New York allowed the FWCRC to move closer to construction by providing professional fees for contract documents for each project. At this point, the house designed by Morris Gutierrez Architects is complete, and six others are ready for construction on sites purchased by the FWCRC.

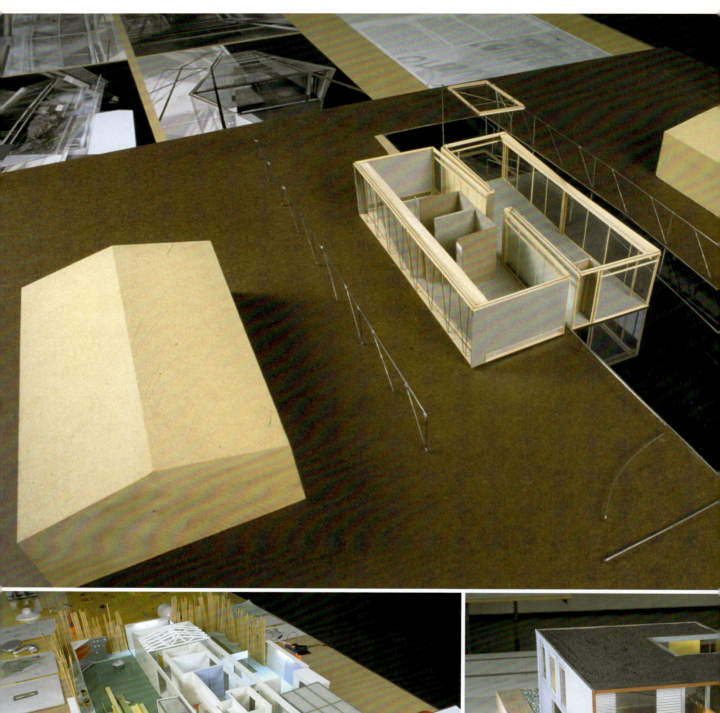
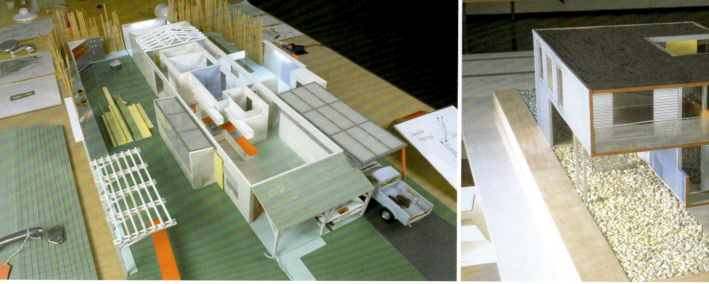

Background

The federal funds made available in 1996 for down-payment voucher programs augmented financial incentives already in place for public-private partnerships in housing development—historic-preservation and low-income tax credits, tax abatements, and donated city land. This combination of incentives has sometimes influenced design decisions: historic-preservation tax credits are often coupled with low-income housing tax credits in a way that lowers development costs while mandating historical housing types. In most cases, however, these incentives have no clear architectural or urban expression, and the development processes usually result in typical speculative housing, with low-level building and design practices.

Voucher programs have moved the point of entry of subsidies to strategic junctures in the development process: the funding arrives when the house is sold, well after the design process is complete, which has had the de facto effect of eliminating the professional services of architects. The housing is essentially market-rate, and the design process virtually nonexistent. This project was initiated, in part, because the appearance of most subsidized housing reflects this elimination of the design process—and fails to reflect the complexity of the political and economic forces at play in the development of housing and the organization of the contemporary city.

Decentralization

Decentralization—on a practical level and as a political concern—proved to be the most enduring issue. While the architectural designs stand alone, and ultimately must operate on a pragmatic level, the question of political consequence remains. The project treads a line between supporting the effort to move federal housing initiatives toward the market and critiquing the substandard quality of market-rate housing in the United States. The projects outline goals and techniques for a type of housing that offers an alternative to the concentration, isolation, and segregation that characterize much federal housing design, while recognizing that market practices have yet to produce an obvious high-quality alternative.

This study is useful as a set of practical proposals, but its real value lies in the degree to which the entire project and the individual works emerged from applying architectural principles to public policy—the projects are literal volumetric and tectonic responses to policy goals. Themes of centrifugal and centripetal space as characteristic of urban form and housing policy—of decentralization—become both practical and symbolic. This group of architects begins what may be a generational movement toward renewing the political purpose of architectural space and production.

None of the works seeks to revive a particular historical genre or form of architecture. Many of the architects rely on a vocabulary of modern architecture, but none focuses on syntactical or formal transformations as a mode of autonomy or self-reference. Several of these architects learned formal syntax as well as transformational strategies from works by John Hejduk and Peter Eisenman (particularly from the publication *Five Architects*), yet in their careers they have opened their work to a broader negotiation of themes of territory and power, and in most cases, this opening has diminished the formal clarity of the works.

This project is steeped in the idea of resistance: the works highlight the unresolved urban and political crisis in housing and, more broadly, address the construction and legislation of social, racial, and economic territories in housing. The project doesn't attempt to reinvent grass-roots political action or the forms of litigation that accompany contentious housing development, but it does test the potential of resistance and engagement under the current conditions of U.S. building practices.

Between 1996 and 1998, the genesis of this approach can be seen in brief passages in essays by Sanford Kwinter and K. Michael Hays. Regarding resistance, Kwinter, in his "Far From Equilibrium" column in *ANY*, described anyone who "still" relied on the "efficacy of negative dialectics" as "gullible." Hays's introduction to *Architecture Theory Since 1968* concluded that a younger audience may have such an "altogether altered" relationship to consumption that its members have become hesitant to engage in a practice that resists the dominant productive economies of the city. Hays suggested that an overt resistance to the commodity processes of labor, material, and financing, which underlie the production of architecture, may no longer hold appeal for younger architects. His coda, unlike Kwinter's, affirms the role of negative dialectics in the face of a significant political and productive crisis, but concludes that the sustained expansion of the United States economy affected the degree to which a new generation sought refuge against the market. The pliability of the formal work in 16 Houses reflects this condition: the architects were working between modes of engagement and resistance, and the houses in turn reveal the strife of their origins.

The goal was, and still is, to view architecture as being enzymatically sustained rather than undermined by urban processes of rationalization, production, and finance—yet also to promote the role of resistance. Each of the works in 16 Houses exhibits both positions. Procedural and temporal ideas of architectural and urban production—systems of management, legislation, and finance, and the role of the state as it protects the market—are given architectural presence.

Text excerpted from 16 Houses: Designing the Public's Private House by Michael Bell.

Glass House @ 2 Degrees

Client Fifth Ward Community Redevelopment Corporation
Site Fifth Ward, Houston, Texas   **Date of Design** 2004
Status Designed   **Budget** $113,000

This nine-hundred-square-foot, single-family house with two bedrooms and two bathrooms was designed for a five-thousand-square-foot lot in Houston's Fifth Ward, the city's lowest-income neighborhood, and commissioned by the Fifth Ward Community Redevelopment Corporation. The project's cost will be subsidized by a federal voucher program that will provide a $9,500 down payment, in hopes of providing a lower-income family with the foundation from which to build a home in the American metropolis. Glass House @ 2 Degrees is imagined as a lens that affords a new view on the city—a tentative, complex, yet powerful grasp on an elusive life.

An ultimately stable and closed structure, Glass House @ 2 Degrees extends its apparent geometric boundaries with transparency and an emerging complexity of torsional stresses that animate and threaten to buckle the planar surfaces of the off-the-rack sliding-glass doors. It is a folded structure—a simple approximation of a continuous surface—with a topology metered by the critical dimensions of mass-produced building components. Its form is a working compromise between philosophy, mathematics, geometry, and production. Six sets of sliding-glass doors measure twenty feet each; the alternate inside-outside panels slide along a planar center of gravity and alter the rotational momentum of the balanced track. The building folds in on itself to form two shallow light wells that illuminate the bedrooms. The two-degree fold results from a push at each corner of the building; the north and south elevations implode at the center.

Glass House @ 2 Degrees is a plate structure—the taut surfaces of tempered glass are pushed to reveal tensions and energies—as well as a repository of energy and the accrued labor of its making. It was one of nine projects awarded a 2001 *Progressive Architecture* design award out of more than four hundred international entries. The project was also shown at the Museum of Modern Art in New York, in an exhibition curated by Terence Riley.

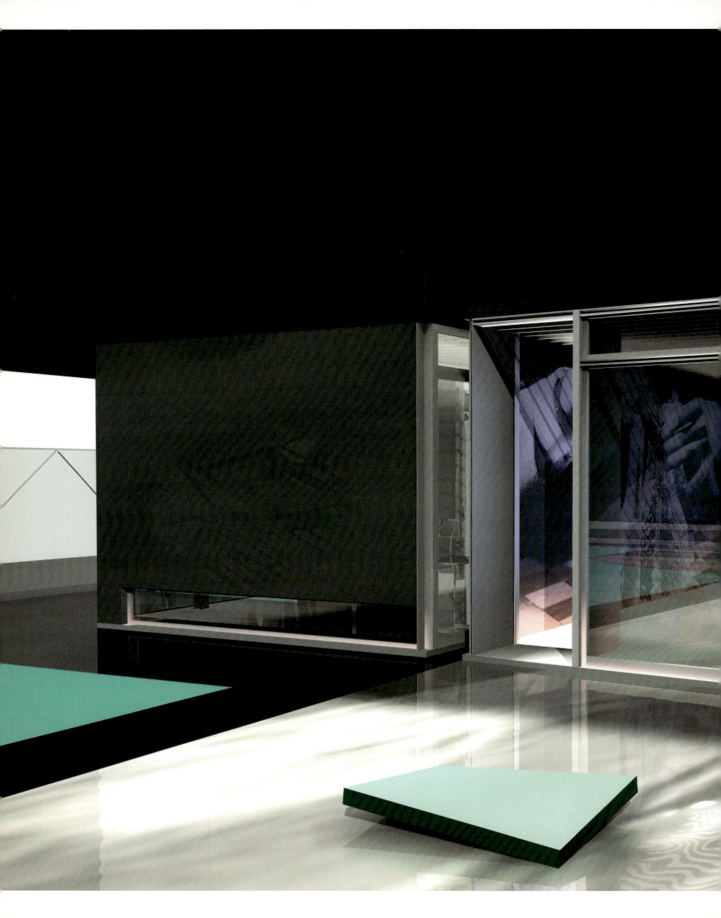

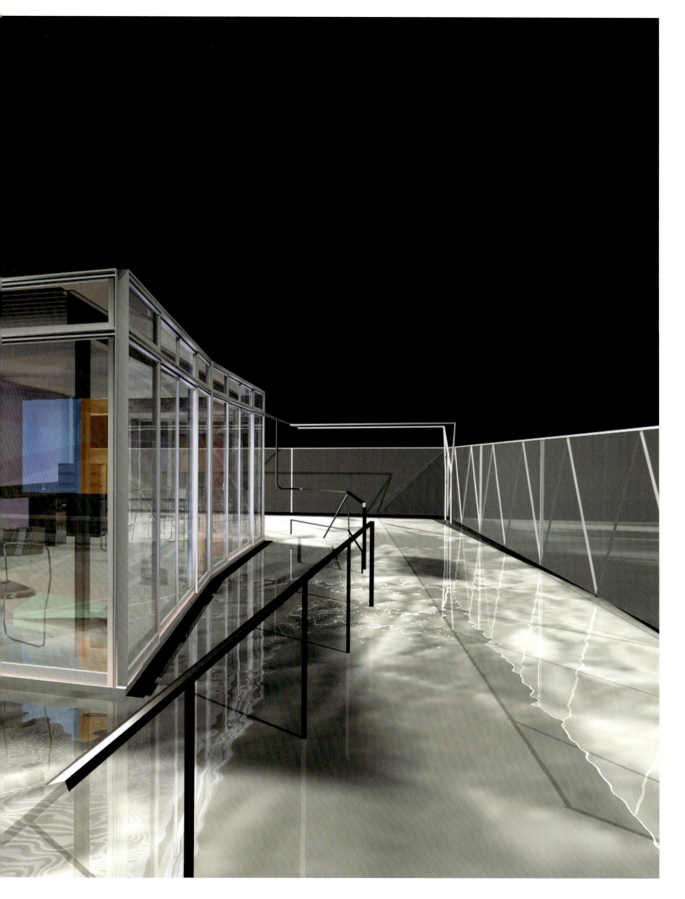

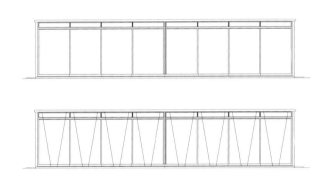

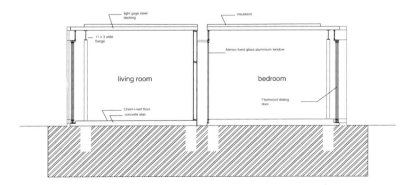

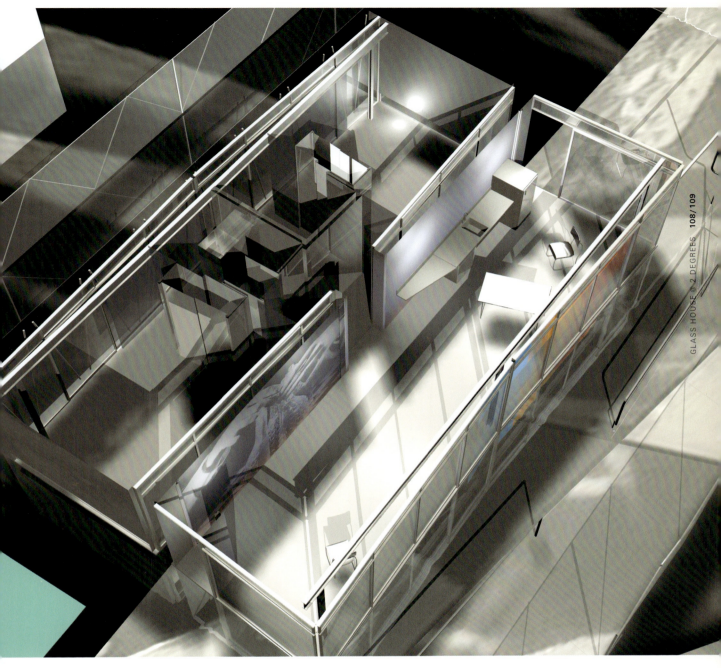

Steel Becomes Aluminum

The steel-and-glass architecture that was conceived around newly refined technologies at the beginning of the twentieth century was at the forefront of a new paradigm in economics and materials production. Today aluminum is generally substituted for steel in the construction of a window section (at Philip Johnson's St. Thomas University in Houston, aluminum windows recently replaced steel, cutting the weight by 75 percent), and consequently the weight and physical momentum of building has changed. The steel-and-glass factories and houses designed in the early twentieth century were produced in a manufacturing economy that, according to the theorist Moishe Postone, took advantage of the capital arrangements of modern factory processes such as divided labor and yet still ideally allowed workers to feel connected to their products. A factory worker could be said to work "in the city" and "for the city." The equation is quasi-territorial: a worker's grounded relation to space, production, and city is balanced by connectivity to family and place, but each component is only partially intact. The relationships between these coordinates could be intuited in what was produced—you could see the city in its artifacts. The politics of this interior—or indeed of working, living, or being in the city of labor—is today almost unilaterally suspect, if not architecturally impossible. Can architecture provide the intuited connection of worker, artifact, and city that Postone's equation suggests? What kind of house would allow you to live in a way that offered a view to the city's complexity? The slightly inflected surfaces of Glass House @ 2 Degrees search for the momentum of the city.

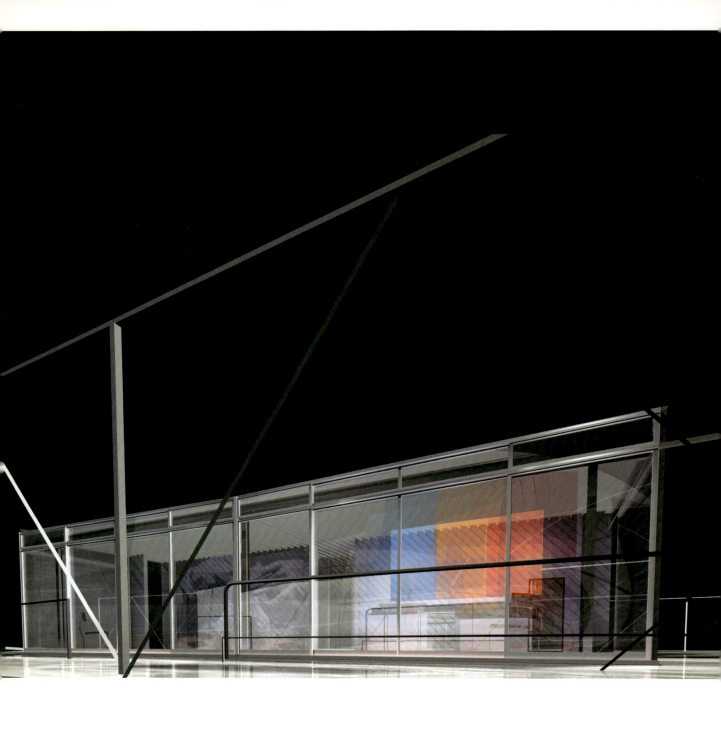

Roof System

The roof system is metal decking with rigid insulation and a polyurethane roof membrane supported by a light-gage steel frame.

Torsion, Bearing, and Time

A push at the corner of the original developer box causes a collapse and a fold, or a crease, in the facade. The sliding-glass doors move in this axis; the house is "broken." The facade crease implies a buckling in the roof surface—a fourth dimension of deformation is added to the otherwise stable three-dimensional form. The house implies dimensions beyond its Cartesian form.

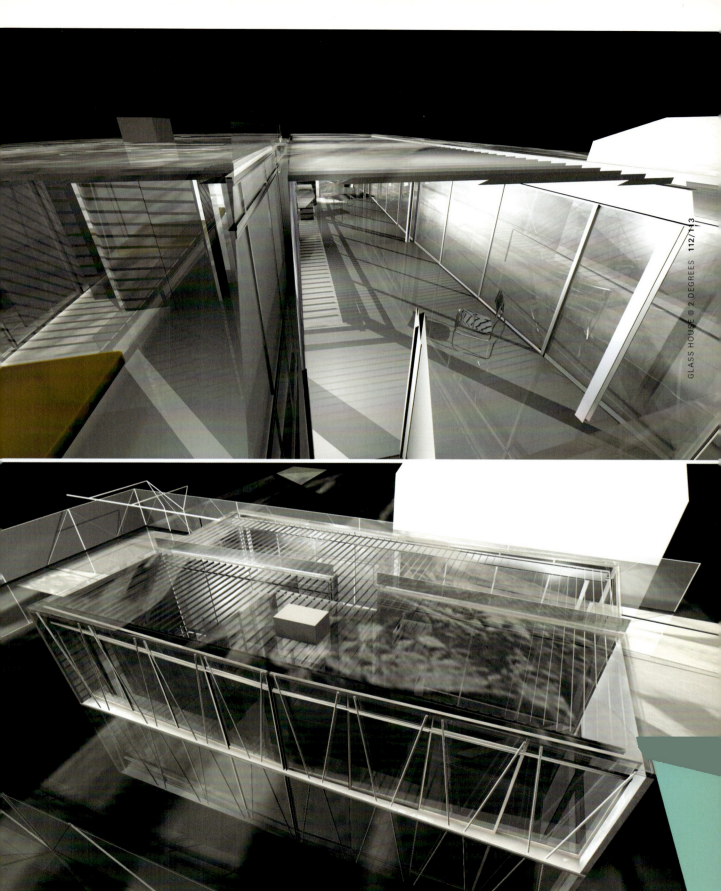

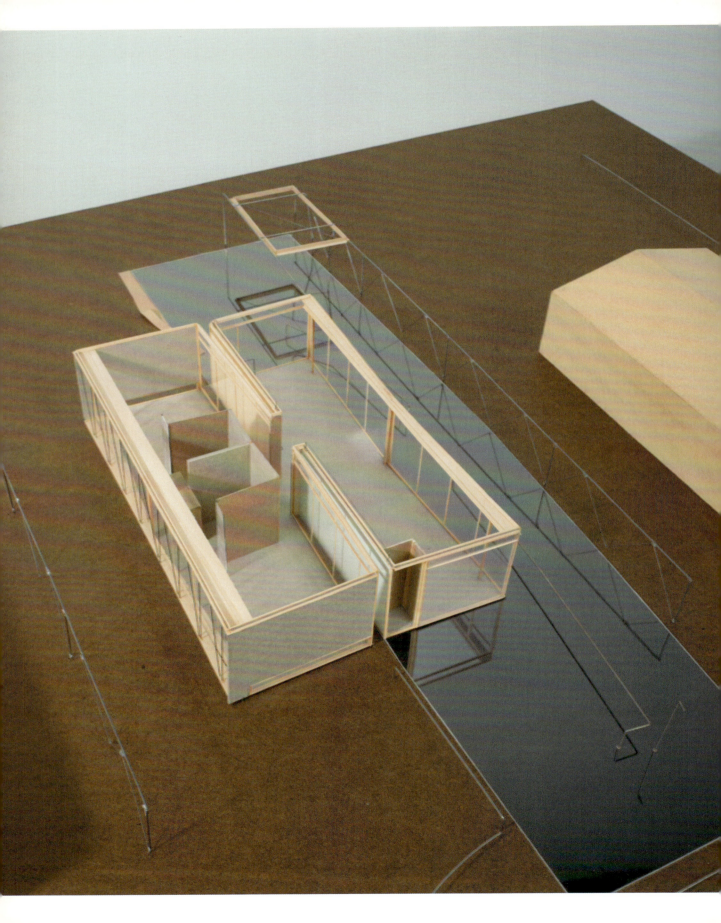

FIG 1 I-59 freeway, Houston, Texas

1 Colin Rowe and Robert Slutzky, "Transparency: Literal and Phenomenal," *Perspecta* 8 (1963).

2 Rowe and Eisenman subsequently became widely influential in urban theory, while Slutzky moved increasingly toward the practice of painting and away from architectural theory. His painting, however, has offered significant if not momentous challenges to the work accomplished with Rowe. Slutzky's architectural design, or his influence on architectural design, is best known in relation to the Diamond Houses and paintings conceived with John Hejduk during the early 1970s. These works were generally accomplished in architecture in relation to plan and orthographic projection: they were not conceived in relation to the same mode of perspectival frontality that was explored in the early essays. In other words, their relation to architectural vision is primarily within the realm of drawing, and they imply a vision for the architect rather than the building occupant. The Diamond Houses promised a new means of generating architectural space, but more important they also proposed a new means of comprehending space by understanding its pictorial techniques.

The Swimmer: Navigating the Inchoate Fabric and the Aftereffects of Economic Promiscuity

In the contemporary metropolis it seems we oscillate on the cusp of two spaces: while fully connected, plugged in, subjugated, over-coded, and prearranged by the mechanisms of urbanism, we are also adrift, loose, and flailing, in the malformed, unshaped spaces that the templates of commodification fail to cohere. In these spaces—adjacent to the freeway, beside the house, behind the retail strip—the trajectory of economic vectors that maintain and invent the shape of the city find nothing to carry or transmit them, let alone give them plastic presence. These spaces slip off of us as water slips in sheets off a swimmer emerging from a pool—wafting, cohering, flexing to, and unfolding from the body. Though the codes of the contemporary city are mediated by the intellect, it is hard to believe that we don't swim in and out of the vaporous, aplastic spaces they construct, that we don't register their haptic presence as they slip on and off.

Introduction: Perspecta's Other Urbanism

RSE is an acronym for Colin Rowe, Robert Slutzky, and Peter Eisenman in the context of *Perspecta,* circa 1971. Rowe and Slutzky's "Transparency: Literal and Phenomenal" was first published in *Perspecta 8* in 1963.[1] Peter Eisenman's essay "From Object to Relationship II: Giuseppe Terragni's Casa Giuliani Frigerio" first appeared in *Perspecta 13–14* in 1971, along with part two of Rowe and Slutzky's "Transparency" articles. RSE is invented shorthand that heuristically conflates the two essays, written in what might be argued to have been a collective manner. Despite the historically decisive nature of both essays, Rowe, Slutzky, and Eisenman opened the door to rewriting the application of their work, particularly in relation to urbanism. As of 1971 all three writers had yet to engage a theory or practice of the city, even as the implications of their work were vulnerable to both the spatial expanse of contemporary urbanism and its ubiquitous financial procedures.[2] Neither "Transparency: Literal and Phenomenal" nor "From Object to Relationship II: Giuseppe Terragni's Casa Giuliani Frigerio" examined the urban implications of its premises, yet each promised and implied themes of a broader and more comprehensive spatial field that was potentially urban or metropolitan in character.

The dispersed urban conditions of present-day cities such as Houston, Los Angeles, or the fringes of metropolitan New York—the latter-day postwar city that was well under way in 1963—coerce new modes of vision from Rowe, Slutzky, and Eisenman's foundational work. Both essays assume an idealized subject discrete from local or actual context. RSE's subject is described as an "observer" without reference to the segregate nature of this position, a viewing subject that is apart from the urban field. Each essay is also predominantly architectural in its concerns. The experience of space is described at the scale of the building and understood through a pictorial reading, one that is subject-originated and frontal. In order to sustain the potential of this early work by RSE, a necessarily less ideal and segregate problem of the viewing subject is described in this essay. The term "observer" is replaced by "visual subject," and vision will be shown to reconcile itself with a broader array of architectural and urban technologies. Architecture and a visual subject are here placed in a broader and less heuristic realm of space and, ultimately, power.

Urban Memory

RSE's visual models find their most significant urban corollary in the mid-1970s writings of Rafael Moneo on Aldo Rossi. Here a potential alternative evolution to the development of vision and frontality in the works of RSE emerges in a theory of vision and memory. A line is drawn through the trajectory of each critic and architect—from Rowe to Rossi—which finds in each participant a unifying but challenging relation to Henri Bergson's theorization of memory and the role of the body in the sustenance and use of memory. An alternative architectural and urban present—a renewed urban subject—is revealed when these foundational architectural histories-theories are reread through Bergson, through each other, and through the vacated spaces of the contemporary city. Bergson's description of memory as a time-image and movement-image, as an intuited presence situated "between a thing itself" and its representation,[3] extends Rowe and Slutzky's themes of phenomenal transparency and Rossi's and Moneo's theorizations of material and memory. It also provides a preface to Eisenman's work on simultaneity and frontality in his analysis of Terragni's Casa Giuliani-Frigerio of 1939, and contextualizes Terragni's earlier optical experiments in photo-elastic stress analysis—work that predates and supports themes in Eisenman's analysis of the later work. Together, these five architect-critics reveal a potential other postwar urban role for what Gyorgy Kepes called the "language of vision."

Part 1: Rossi's Technological Amnesia

In his 1976 essay "Aldo Rossi: The Idea of Architecture and the Modena Cemetery," Rafael Moneo implied that the foundations of Rossi's theoretical purpose relied on a self-imposed amnesia. Moneo claimed that Rossi had to adopt an "evasive" relation to broader urban technologies to secure the authority of architecture in the postwar city. Rossi's architecture was "deliberately forgetting the framework of the real, even at levels evident and compromised as the technological one," wrote Moneo.[4] To the reader, it seemed that Moneo was seeking the grounds to support Rossi, but the evidence of the contemporary city—the late twentieth-century metropolis—made Rossi's propositions difficult to accept without reservations.

Moneo's essay began a process of reconciling Rossi's theory and practice of architecture within a broader and ultimately more self-sustaining field, in this case the postwar city of Western Europe and the United States. If Rossi's amnesia sought to protect the authority and autonomy of architecture from a metropolis characterized as both predatory and vicarious, Moneo's essay constituted a turning point. In addressing the self-sustaining role of the metropolis itself,[5] Moneo seemed reluctant to accept a project of architectural autonomy and instead came close to proposing the autonomy of the metropolis as a fiscal, governmental, and power-laden instrument. One could say the foundations of Moneo's own work were established in this cleft. Moneo's work from that date forward continually tests rather than affirms the autonomy of architecture, as it seeks the dimensions and material facts in the construction of urban subjectivity.

Moneo described Rossi's urban theories as a mode of temporal vision, one that can be aligned with Henri Bergson's theory of duration and the temporal aspects of his theory of intuition and memory. In Rossi's work, architecture offered what Moneo termed a "fleeting glimpse" of the city achieved in the suspension of analytic technique. Rossi's own writing, as is well known, proposed

FIG 2 Fifth Ward, Houston, Texas
FIG 3 The swimmer

3 Henri Bergson, *Matter and Memory* (New York: Zone Books, 1988), 9. See also *Nobel Lectures, Literature, 1901–1967*, vol. 1 (Amsterdam: Elsevier Publishing Company, 1970).
4 Rafael Moneo, "Aldo Rossi: The Idea of Architecture and the Modena Cemetery," *Oppositions* (Summer 1976): 9.
5 See Massimo Cacciari, "The Dialectics of the Negative and the Metropolis," in *Architecture and Nihilism: On the Philosophy of Modern Architecture* (New Haven: Yale University Press, 1993), 7. Cacciari's description of the metropolis is essential: "We are still in the *city*," writes Cacciari, "as long as we are in the presence of use values alone, or in the presence of the simple production of the commodity, or if the two instances stand next to each other in a non-dialectical relation. Whereas we are in the *metropolis* when production assumes its own social rationale, when it determines the modes of consumption and succeeds in making them function toward the renewal of the cycle."

6 Moneo, "Aldo Rossi," 5.
7 Gilles Deleuze, *Bergson-ism* (New York: Zone Books, 1988), 77.
8 Bergson, *Matter and Memory*, 179.
9 Bergson, *Matter and Memory*, 180.

that buildings found their fullest urban meaning as a form of passive and undirected memory. This mode of memory was not attached to an active or strategic process of remembering; it was instead an unregulated and more ambient theory of memory as afterimage no longer authored by the demonstrative needs of its host or limited by the position of the host's body. For Rossi, the afterimage was understood to "construct the city"—it was a way to *see* the city, and allowed the full comprehension of the city from the relative isolation of a subject's singular vantage. Architecture in this equation was less than literal, yet more than phenomenal, in Rowe and Slutzky's terms. More so, it was greater than a representation. Architecture as memory, as time-image, allowed Rossi to conceive of architecture as fixed, finite, and discrete, yet also relieved it of its relative and artificial, or overly local, unity. If architecture was to be "a great representation of the human condition" even in its "fixed" literalness, memory allowed its subject to become urban within a wider field, yet remain rooted in the isolation and sight of a subject.[6] Bergson's theorizing of duration often parallels Rossi's theory of memory. For Bergson, the multiple and temporal comprehensions of movement both maintain and supersede the closure of the literal limits of form, the body, and location. "We perceive that being is. . .the very numerous durations"; our own duration is "caught between more dispersed durations and more taut, more intense durations." One moment is thus "extended to the whole of the universe," writes Bergson.[7]

For Rossi, memory provided access to a dispersed world and an extended sense of time and continuity. Bergson's, and one could say Rossi's, architectural as well as human body is limited in mechanical extension, yet is always turned toward desired action even in its stillness. The body provides the essential "function to limit. . . the life of the spirit" and "indicates the parts and aspects of matter on which we can lay hold."[8] The body is local, and as such is overwhelmed by the movement and technologies of systems beyond its own boundaries. As the literal site of perception and subsequent memory, however, Bergson's body is prepared for action by continually altered degrees of memory. For both Bergson and Rossi, memory is defined in gradients of direct or strategic usefulness. "Pure memory," writes Bergson, is a "nascent sensation" and "not essentially localized in any point of the body." Bergson's body, sited in actual space like Rossi's, "ceaselessly" presses to extend its own limits; it relies on memory to open "the door which the body" has left half open.[9] Memory in both cases extends the closure and finitude of circumstances created beyond the local authority of the subject.

For Rossi it extended the essential role of architecture in construction of urban subjectivity, and it allowed him to imagine an autonomous role for architecture in the context of a technologically predatory city.

RSE: Phenomenal Memory, Literal Form

Colin Rowe and Robert Slutzky's "Transparency: Literal and Phenomenal" and Peter Eisenman's "From Object to Relationship II: Giuseppe Terragni's Casa Giuliani-Frigerio" offer a parallel to this theme of competing, but not exclusive, relations between contradictory readings of space or location. Rowe and Slutzky's essay opens with a reference to Gyorgy Kepes's analysis of overlapping and simultaneous figures in cubist painting. Kepes proposed that the overlapping quality of forms common in cubism gave presence to a new "optical quality," one that allows the simultaneity of competing readings of space without an "optical destruction" of either reading. In placing RSE's work in the context of Bergson's and Rossi's theories of memory, the dialectic themes of cubist visual techniques, such as overlapping and simultaneity, are given new dimension and means of transformation. RSE's thesis of visual subjectivity is given more multivalent potential; as such the discretely located visual subject suffers less in insisting its origin in the comprehension of space, and memory coupled with vision extends the boundaries of circumstance.

In the contemporary city, a project of architecture based on form, figure, or material is troubled by the degree to which the dimensional attributes of these urban realms have historically been understood in static terms. In this essay, architecture is understood as an adjunct of managed capital, or in a broader sense, as a result of commodity or temporal computational systems. Far from classical ideals of timelessness, architecture produced by the market systems that dominate the contemporary city is indeed embedded with time-based processes of material and labor, yet these modes of time are rarely knowable or recoverable in the final form of building—the memory of the city's production is essentially inaccessible. As such, architecture finds itself in a dialectic relation with the wider field of the city. It seems to stand in opposition to the city. While architecture is derived from traceable processes and from market techniques and needs, the market remains unrecoverable in the visual, optic, or plastic evidence of architecture. The contemporary city compounds this scenario: what, one may ask, are we looking at when we look at the city—what do we find in its expanse and how could architecture help cohere this field?

The techniques of literal and phenomenal space described by Rowe and Slutzky have ceased to operate as the "critical instruments" they sought in the wider field of the city. More important, they have ceased to fully describe the relations of power and territory that conflate in contemporary urban and visual subjectivity, either in relation to pictorial space or to financial and material spaces. Yet the goals of Rowe and Slutzky and Moneo and Rossi remain strategically essential; like Bergson, each of these critics and architects offers processes of immanent as well as actual formalization. The theories of RSE were intended, as Bergson would have it, to "transcend space without stepping out from extensivity."[10] Each critic gives architecture dimensions beyond its discrete or literal limits, even as the literal limits are didactically enunciated. Each anticipated a wider urban field, but as of 1971 had not yet speculated on its formation, in part to sustain the project of architectural autonomy.[11]

Eisenman's Terragni

Peter Eisenman supplemented "From Object to Relationship II: Giuseppe Terragni's Casa Giuliani-Frigerio" with diagrams drawn in part by Daniel Libeskind. The analysis presented what Eisenman called a "conceptual ambiguity" developed from the simultaneous use of the "two opposing conceptions of space" manifest in plan but understood frontally via elevation.[12] Eisenman's analysis depicted both concepts as simultaneously at work in the Casa Giuliani-Frigerio. The effect was to leave the origin of the building's spatial energy uncertain, while maintaining a sense of potential and immanent, or one might say phenomenal, energy. At times Eisenman came close to revealing a theory of vision linked to matter that is similar to Bergson's theory of intuition, in which architecture instigates what Bergson called two fluxes contained and held temporarily within a

FIG 4 Giuseppe Terragni, Casa Giuliani-Frigerio, 1939–40

10 Bergson, *Matter and Memory,* 10.
11 Rowe's work in urban theory and design began in 1980 and was laid out in his book *Collage City,* written with Fred Koetter. Eisenman's work in urbanism began in the mid-1980s; today the division between urban and architectural work in Eisenman's practice is indistinguishable in terms of a figure-ground. Both Rowe and Eisenman essentially turned to history when they began to directly address urbanism. They also turned to history as it reveals itself in plan more so than in elevation. Both Rowe and Slutzky allowed the role of architectural frontality to diminish in their critical work after these essays were written, as Eisenman did in his practice. The role of the facade not only diminished in their work as they turned their attention to urbanism—so too did the role of a visual subject other than the architect. Rowe proposed an urban planning by way of the collage techniques of adjacency. Like his theories of transparency, these were in part derived from cubism and themes of juxtaposition and contingency, but they were mostly administered as a form of planning—they

were thought of horizontally, and the visual subject was the architect who witnessed their form in plan. Eisenman allowed site and local or historical adjacent forms to enter the transformation procedures that he had used to create his earlier independent and essentially physically site-less works of architecture. Again, this influence was predominantly accomplished in plan; even as Eisenman's early work on Terragni was based on a reading of space gained from elevation, one could say his work on urbanism was at its outset related predominantly to plan. Rowe also provided an intellectual context for work on historical urban and architectural type by Rob Krier and wrote an essay, "A.D. Profile 20: Roma Interrotta," ed. and trans. Jennifer Franchina, *Architectural Design* 49, nos. 3–4 (1979).

12 The first considered space as centripetal and seeking a central origin. This concept was understood to produce space in a subtractive manner; mass is seen as cut away from a preexisting solid. The second concept of space is shown to be centrifugal in nature, a planar layering that tended outward from an assumed yet uncertain peripheral origin.

13 Deleuze, *Bergsonism*, 80.

14 In the United States, themes of duration and memory as instigated by

third duration. Bergson, like Eisenman, relies on the term simultaneity in his description of these multiple durations. "Such is our first idea of simultaneity," writes Bergson. "We call simultaneous, then, two external fluxes that occupy the same duration because they hold each other in the duration of the third." Bergson's duration includes that of the viewer: "Our own simultaneity of fluxes … brings us back to internal duration, to real duration."[13] Eisenman's reading can be understood as a form of this duration: it creates a third form that encapsulates the expansion and contraction of two types of space and implies that the subject and object are fused in a third perceptual space.

In his analysis, Eisenman moves the subject's frontal comprehension of space from the actual, and thereby relative, vantage point to the represented, and thereby intuited, understanding of the whole work. In doing so he places both the subject and the object within a third duration—a third field—that allows the autonomy of each participant, yet also allows presence only through the other body. Eisenman's interest in the "ambiguity," or the conceptual relations between competing spatial readings, in Terragni's architecture was intended to reveal an autonomy founded in this ambiguity: architecture resists a static and foreclosed finitude as it evades easy reading and definitive origins. In the context of the contemporary city this autonomy has been potentially inverted: it is the autonomy of financial and material processes achieved in their dexterity that Moneo feared Rossi was not acknowledging, and that today render most buildings inadvertently autonomous.

Part 2: Terragni and Lingeri's Photo-elastic Experiments

Eisenman's analysis of the work of Giuseppe Terragni marked the arrival of Eisenman's tremendous influence on architectural and cultural criticism. However, it can also be understood as a turning point that made other, more culturally dominant modes of linguistic criticism not only possible, but perhaps inevitably more influential. The project of linguistics itself and the application of language theories to architecture became the central foundation for more prevalent architectures, such as those of Robert A. M. Stern and Michael Graves, which made the themes broadly accessible.[14] Eisenman's work has not entered and perhaps never desired to enter the stream of general urban commodity or media processes, as has the work of Graves or Stern. It may now be possible to suggest that the linguistic trajectories represented on one hand by Eisenman and on another by Stern have suppressed the technical aspects of material and mechanical properties, or knowingly interpreted their prevalence from an existential position. Eisenman's work on Terragni is an essential yet unrealized key to Terragni's earlier work on photo-elasticity—a process that Terragni employed in the structural analysis of his proposal for the design of Palazzo Littorio in 1934. Terragni, with partner Pietro Lingeri, used a set of photo-elastic stress analysis models while designing Palazzo Littorio Solution A in the early 1930s, a work preceding Casa Giuliani-Frigerio by five years. Terragni's work in photo-elasticity links themes of transparency in the work of Rowe and Slutzky, and material and memory in the work of Moneo and Rossi. More important, it predates the Casa Giuliani-Frigerio—the building of Eisenman's analysis—and suggests that the conceptions of space described by Eisenman could not have been possible if not for these early experiments. Terragni's work in optics is more extensive than has been historically noted.[15]

Terragni's work on photo-elasticity literally conflates themes of classical visual subjectivity with materials and themes of technology and industry. In the context of RSE, vision revealed a structure of conceptual relationships that "accrue to relationships between objects, rather than to the physical presence of the objects themselves." The photo-elastic process *is* based in the physical presence of the objects themselves—it is matter that one is seeing, and this seeing is achieved as a conflation of classical perspective and chemical engineering and lens techniques. It marked the description of a twentieth century mode of vision and a visual subject for whom vision and duration are linked in a seeing of material and technological processes that imbue the architectural and urban space of the contemporary city.[16]

To date, the most significant attempt to place the role of Terragni and Lingeri's work in photo-elasticity is in Manfredo Tafuri's essay "Giuseppe Terragni: Subject and Mask."[17] The essay questions the aberration these tests seem to represent in Terragni's career, but does not examine the intrinsic properties of photo-elastic processes themselves. Tafuri is forced to reconcile their significance in the design of Palazzo Littorio within the linguistic prerogatives that dominated the trajectory of his own critical writing. Tafuri was unable to synthesize his linguistic research and his sometimes startling structural and mechanical insights. His analysis was at times surprising in its insight and in the degree to which it intuitively sensed the potential implications of the photo-elastic work. For example, while Tafuri recognizes that what he called the "wall" that composes the primary facade is actually a "box-like structure," he did not recognize that this reading changes not just the mechanics of its cantilever and its rotational tendencies, but also the facade's ability to "speak " or be "read" (in Tafuri's words). Tafuri's critique concludes by stating that he is unsure why the isostatic lines of the photo-elastic process are represented on the proposed final surface of the building.[18] His analysis concludes instead that Terragni had reduced these "forces" to an "arabesque," to an "apodictic word." The building was thus forced to be understood as "speechless" and "silent" and, as such, ultimately corroborated Tafuri's existential interpretation. Had Tafuri examined the history and implications of the photo-elastic process, he may have concluded that Terragni's intentions were instead to open architecture's visual techniques to new instruments and new means and to thus transform the visual subject's relation to technology and power. Tafuri also suggested that the shallow curve of the structure was not sufficient to define the piazza in front of Palazzo Littorio, without noting its role in providing a mechanical ballast or stiffness to the suspended structure.

There were, of course, pragmatic needs for the photo-elastic analysis: the scale of the cantilever that Terragni and Lingeri proposed in Solution A necessitated that the architects test the potential stress and strain in the proposed structure. Had Tafuri situated Terragni and Lingeri's ambitions within the techniques of the photo-elastic process itself—the science and optics of these techniques were being perfected as the building was designed—he would have potentially diminished the role of linguistics in his conclusions and have unanchored a project of frontality from a project of linguistics and semiotics. An examination of the photo-elastic process itself would have transferred the role of a linguistic, or sign-based, critique to an inquiry instead focused on perspectivalism, optics, lens-camera mechanisms, and chemistry and material mechanics. The final mode of subjectivity would have been one of visual subjectivity linked to

Aldo Rossi found counterparts in a different and essentially more linguistic mode of memory, or remembering. Semiotic and historical trajectories conceived by Robert Venturi and Denise Scott Brown, Robert A. M. Stern, and Michael Graves, among others, gained wider appeal and easier application to the commodity processes that are at the heart of United States market practices. These practices dominate the latter-day metropolis' eventual form. In a market- and media-based economy, the works of Venturi, Scott Brown, Stern, and Graves entered the very bloodstream of communications and began a process of suturing the inchoate fabric of a United States terrain vague with a network of semiotic bridges—the city was reconceived as a linguistic artery connected by signs rather than material. If economic practices had rendered a vacant postwar metropolis, it was possible to rebuild it with the sign systems of media.

15 See Noam Chomsky, *Syntactic Structures* (The Hague: Mouton and Co., 1965), 16. The foundation for Eisenman's analysis was influenced by the early linguistic research of Noam Chomsky on the potential of "deep structure." In the context of Chomsky's research, the term "deep structure" described the underlying

rules and relationships that constitute an essential yet not necessarily transparent or visible grammar. Through deep structure an infinite set of syntactic transformations could be generated: "The deep structure of a syntactic description determines its semantic interpretation," wrote Chomsky, but there may not necessarily be any similarities between the surface and deep structure of a linguistic or formal appearance. In fact, such relationships may "manifest sharp incongruencies between the visible surface structure and its deep structure of underlying relations." Eisenman proposed that the search for an architectural syntax was likely to be found in the ambiguity between these conceptual and actual relationships—the syntax was to be found in the condition that was essentially temporal and based in the flux between more stable realms.

16 Richard C. Dove and Paul H. Adams, *Experimental Stress Analysis and Motion Measurement* (Columbus, Ohio: C. E. Merrill Books, 1964), 288.

17 Manfredo Tafuri, "Giuseppe Terragni: Subject and Mask," trans. Diane Ghirardo, *Oppositions* (Winter 1977): 1–25.

18 Tafuri, "Giuseppe Terragni," 6.

FIG 5 Palazzo Littorio, Solution A, 1934: the pattern of the photo-elastic process is revealed in the proposed building surface; the center cutaway would provide a speaking platform for Mussolini to address his audience

material intuition, and the role of the architect would have migrated toward a realm of newly acquired visual and technical procedures. With this change, the existential dimensions of Tafuri's critique might have been forced to migrate as well, toward a subject whose comprehension of visual depth and space would have technological dimensions.

The photo-elastic tests by Terragni and Lingeri were done to ensure equilibrium as the necessary and final state in the design of the massive cantilever of Solution A. In choosing to represent the residual and latent forces—the surplus energies—at work in the creation of this political spectacle, Terragni and Lingeri created a visual critique of metropolitan dialectics. In doing so, they also created a crisis in the arena of metropolitan subjectivity. This vertical surface is an expansive visual field that delivers to Mussolini the pictorial gaze of an audience whose subjectivity it both conscripts and ironically severs. In transforming the perspectival depth of a viewing subject into the thermodynamic modeling of light as a material strain within photography, Terragni and Lingeri effectively flattened the distance that segregates subject and object or subject from spectacle. In other words, it is possible to read this pictorial field as expanded and also foreclosed or quite literally foreshortened. In essence, this delimiting of the pictorial field *is* the architecture of Palazzo Littorio.[19] It forms an artificial contrivance and the model of nature's duration—a frontalized and at least partially classicized architectural design whose structural mechanics instigate a migratory set of forces that mimic the duration and temporary nature of organic life. Tafuri's attempt to analyze Palazzo Littorio asked what these forces represent and indeed whether they were intended to represent anything at all. I would instead suggest that they were intended not to represent but to create a new horizon for architectural space, based on the intuitive as well as literal comprehension of material and mechanical duration. In doing so, they renew our own duration in relation to material and the power relations inherent in material production. Here, architectural frontality and perspectival design are involved with and reveal modes of space and power that have dominated the twentieth-century fabrications of capital, power, and political authority. Can these modes of vision be applied to a visual comprehension of the postwar or contemporary city?

Part 3: Preserving the Phenomenal

Like Eisenman, Rowe and Slutzky began their work with a dialectic pairing of apparently competing tendencies—transparency examined in literal as well as phenomenal terms. For Rowe and Slutzky, the theme of transparency led initially to a didactic reading of unresolved contradictions: transparency is a key theme of simultaneity, yet it does not always reveal content or origins, thereby affording a form of ambiguity. Rowe and Slutzky describe literal transparency as a "quality of substance as in a glass curtain wall." Conceptually, however, the main goal of the essay was to reveal the potential usefulness of phenomenal transparency. Here the term may mean "an inherent quality of organization," an understanding rather than a revelation of orders. In this second reading the term "transparent" ceases to be "that which is perfectly clear" and becomes instead "that which is clearly ambiguous." The distinction laid the groundwork for a potential uncharted realm of phenomenal perception that Rowe and Slutzky left unexplored. Indeed, they warned against a hasty exploration or delineation of this form of space, stating at the conclusion of

19 The photo-elastic work of Terragni and Lingeri delimited the mechanical as well as physical axes of materials used in the model; the model was less complex than the building proposal. The model concentrated events at a crossroads where the distress of the material would reveal itself. The polarization of the light waves that allow the photo-elastic process to be recorded limits the visible waves of the spectrum; the complexity of deformation in the model is also limited to the plane. This dialectic modeling, on one hand, limits the usefulness of the results, but it also reduces the complexity of techniques at play and thereby sets the stage for the less complex comprehension of the movement than would occur in the actual building. The model does not reveal the full complexity of stress and strain. Nonetheless it linked the comprehension of material properties to those of vision and set the stage for a form of visual duration.

20 Robert Slutzky with Joan
Ockman, "Color/Structure/
Painting," *Robert Slutzky
15 Paintings, 1980–1984*
(San Francisco: Modernism
Gallery, 1984), unpaginated.
Also contains essays by
John Hejduk, Dore Ashton,
and Alberto Sartoris.

"Transparency: Literal and Phenomenal" that they intended only to reveal that there were two species of transparency, and that it would be advantageous not to confuse them. RSE concluded with a proposition that the ambiguous held potentials that neither apparently polar conditions nor less ambiguous positions could fulfill. The ambiguous relation offered a promise of immanent discovery—the boundaries of the literal were extended.

Slutzky's Topologies and the Post-Phenomenal Space

The trajectory of both "Transparency: Literal and Phenomenal" and "From Object to Relationship II: Giuseppe Terragni's Casa Giuliani-Frigerio" has largely been left unexamined with regard to any fundamental criticism of their near canonical stature. Slutzky, however, offered an extension of the theories launched in "Transparency: Literal and Phenomenal" in a 1984 essay cowritten with Joan Ockman entitled "Color/Structure/Painting," published as part of the catalog to his exhibition "Robert Slutzky, 15 Paintings."[20] Slutzky and Ockman's description of a series of paintings by Slutzky depicts a layering of space that is consistent with theories in earlier essays by RSE and with Slutzky's education under Josef Albers at Yale. What is not consistent in the work is the introduction of what Slutzky and Ockman refer to as an oculus—in literal terms, the centralized square painted in the same hue as the torus-shaped periphery of the compositions. The oculus is common across the collection of paintings. Slutzky and Ockman refer to this oculus as a "counter-eye" that confronts "the artist and spectator alike." According to "Color/Structure/Painting," the oculus turns "space inside-out" and, "like a torus-glove," makes "figure and field ambiguously one." The counter-eye instigates a transformation of the painting's frontality, and conversely of vision's role in the positioning of the self as the origin and object of space. These paintings reconfigure their initial field, and the field occupied by the viewer, in a processional unfolding of space that at one level is didactically willful even as the results remain ineffable. Slutzky's pictorial mechanics remain firmly within dialectics; indeed, the spatial ambiguity these paintings instigate relies on the canvas as an originary surface. Slutzky also still posits his subject—at least temporarily—as the origin of the spatial field, before undoing this origin, in some sense plastically unloading it. Though essentially menaced by these initial structures, Slutzky's oculus under duress offers an intuitive grasp of the inferable, a chance to seize and then occupy space, to walk into space and away from the composition's topologically transformed surface. Here we leave the relative and enter the expanded field, but not prior to a crisis in which anticipated spatial relationships are challenged and cataclysmically transformed.

While Rowe and Eisenman each moved on toward proposals for an urbanism based either in collage or historical transformation, it is possible to suggest that both relinquished the role vision might have played if it had followed an evolutionary path from their seminal work. In other words, had RSE's discoveries in visual subjectivity been applied to an urban rather than architectural visual subject, it is possible that the city could have coerced a new mode of vision, derived in part from operations that extend the early work of RSE, as Slutzky advanced it in his painting. The postwar city would be comprehended and *seen* not as a newly reconstructed historical type—a mechanical, pictorial, or historical form—but instead as a phenomenal comprehension of urban form, one produced by dominant techniques of capital, production, material, and commodity practices as well as new means of communication. When literal transparency predominates, it seems possible to claim that architecture finds itself exacerbated by the predominance of the city. When phenomenal transparency predominates, it seems possible to claim for a viewing subject an emergent, undefined, and potentially useful space.

Part 4: Smooth or Negative

At the crucible of this scenario, K. Michael Hays and Sanford Kwinter provide a polar basis for negotiating a new realm not for transparency, but for an urban subject defined in relation to commodity processes and infrastructural technologies—between the economic and technical practices of urbanism. Their texts, published between 1996 and 1998, revealed in each theorist a slightly personal dimension, leaving a mutual strife undeclared, yet palpable. The passages were brief but pungent, implicating each other and the participants within each milieu. Hays's introduction to *Architecture Theory Since 1968*[21] concluded with the acknowledgment that a younger audience may have such an "altogether altered" relationship to consumption that they may be hesitant to engage in practices that resist the dominant productive economies of the city. Hays suggested that an overt resistance to the commodity processes that underlie an entire generation of theorists and practitioners whose work rests upon the negative dialectics of Theodor Adorno was under tremendous criticism, in part due to the pervasiveness and growth of capital economies in the 1990s. The production of architecture based in the work of Adorno and intellectual descendants such as Manfredo Tafuri or Massimo Cacciari, Hays wrote, may no longer hold appeal for younger architects. In a response that was left rhetorically undirected to any particular architect, critic, or theorist, but whose target was clearly Hays and the realm of critics who base their work in Adorno, Sanford Kwinter, in his "Far from Equilibrium" column in *ANY,* was more blunt. Kwinter described anyone who "still" relied on the "efficacy of negative dialectics" as "gullible"; "what matters is infrastructure," he wrote.[22] Kwinter claimed that "form and architecture can no longer make the slightest historical claim on our attention." For Hays, and for a generation of critics and architects who had relied on an intellectual lineage connecting Adorno and Tafuri, the sea change expressed here is epic in scale. Hays's coda suggested that the role of negative dialectics and the preservation of the unrevealed remain useful in the face of the significant political and productive crisis in both urbanism and architecture, but more important, within the culture. I personally agree. The sustained expansion of the United States economy and the absence of a significant Socialist counterpoint affected the degree to which a new generation sought refuge from or options within the market. As both a practical and philosophical position, the tendency toward engagement was increasingly palpable during the 1990s. Here is the potential locus where the term phenomenal might renew its meaning in architecture and urbanism. In rejecting the conclusion that "form is the only rightful end of architectural propositions," Kwinter supported his long-term agenda to move architectural and urban criticism toward theories of movement and change. Kwinter, in effect, negates form itself and its subsequent role as the host to and generator of crisis within Adorno's dialectics. Without form, one need not resort to negation.[23] In reexamining the work of RSE through a lens afforded by Bergson, the dichotomy of Kwinter's and Hays's positions is at least partially alleviated—the dialectics

21 K. Michael Hays, ed., *Architecture Theory Since 1968* (Cambridge, MA: MIT Press, 1998), xiv.

22 Sanford Kwinter, "Playboys of the Western World," *ANY* 13 (1996): 62.

23 "Freedom can be defined in negation only. Corresponding to the concrete form of a specific unfreedom." Theodor W. Adorno, *Negative Dialectics* (New York: Continuum, 1995), 231.

of location and origins of space is maintained, yet it ceases to be the cause of persecution. Bergson's memory is a subject-originated practice, yet it does not require negative practices because it is able to account for change and for newly extensive limits beyond the body's location.

Eyes in the Heat

The Casa Giuliani-Frigerio is perhaps the closest Terragni ever came to eradicating the vestige of perspectivalism and frontality in his work, and it exemplifies a phase of design in which Terragni effectively detached the comprehension of form from vision. In doing so, he clarified the spatial potential of material-matter itself, bringing to a cognitive level an ideal of material duration as a replacement for perspectival relativity. This model has surprising relevance today in looking at the contemporary city. This is the exacerbated realm from which a contemporary application of writings by Rowe, Slutzky, and Eisenman can advance in relation to Terragni and Lingeri's photo-elastic research. The facade of Palazzo Littorio is quite literally a "suppression of depth" and a "contracting of space," as well as a defining of "light sources." Far from a mode of negative criticism or Rossian amnesia, it is an alternative evolution for the role of vision in the work of RSE and within the broad array of technologies that architectural production has yet to address in its dealings with the contemporary city.

"Eyes in the Heat: RSE" first appeared in *Perspecta 34, The Yale Journal of Architecture,* edited by Noah Biklen.

Stateless Housing

Planning Michael Bell Architecture **Architectural Design** Michael Bell
Architecture, Marble Fairbanks Architects, Mark Rakatansky Studio
Client Architectural League of New York (Rosalie Genevro, Executive
Director) in collaboration with the New York Department of Housing,
Preservation, and Development (James Lima, Assistant Commissioner)
Site Arverne Urban Renewal Area, New York **Date of Design** 2001
Status Designed

Stateless Housing is a research and design project focused on the
Arverne Urban Renewal Area—308 acres on the Rockaway Peninsula cleared in the mid-1960s—which is currently the largest tract of
open land in New York City. It was funded in response to developer
proposals submitted to the New York Department of Housing,
Preservation, and Development in response to a request for proposals (RFP). The RFP called for the development of market-rate, two-
family housing on the hundred-acre site, which is surrounded by
three kinds of state-assisted housing: Ocean Village, built by the
Urban Development Corporation; the Arverne Houses, developed
by the Housing Authority of New York; and Hammel Houses, a
Mitchell-Lama housing project. Stateless Housing tests the limits of
architecture in the redevelopment of disinvested territories. The project was exhibited at the Urban Center in Manhattan in the fall of
2001 and at the Yale School of Architecture in the spring of 2002,
alongside proposals by teams from Yale University, City College of
New York, and CASE, an Amsterdam-based research collective
funded by the Dutch government.

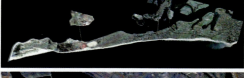

Precedent and Research

The Rockaway Peninsula is home to approximately thirty-eight thousand households, more than thirteen thousand of them in publicly funded and assisted buildings. Ocean Village is on the eastern perimeter of the site at Beach 59th Street; it was built between 1968 and 1974 and offers subsidized housing to lower-income families. At the western perimeter of the site, the Arverne and Hammel houses have an average household income of $13,406 (as of January 1, 1999). Also on the western edge of the site are nine mid-rise slabs—cooperative apartments that are owned by their residents. The NYHPD currently proposes adding as many as two thousand units of new market-rate housing to the area. While these units will not be subsidized at the point of sale, they will be subsidized indirectly through a public-private partnership; the HPD will effectively donate the property to whichever developer is awarded the contract. Major funding for infrastructure is anticipated from the State of New York, which will further reduce development costs.

Double Housing

New development in the area has primarily taken the form of duplex and flat-style housing. In most cases, public-private partnerships have produced quasi-vernacular forms of housing offered for sale instead of rent. The housing often provides two apartments as a single dwelling called a "two-family house": the owner occupies the upper-level flat and rents a lower-level unit for income. These images show the small-scale and generally developer-level of design and materials common in the new publicly supported housing being offered for sale.

Federal Housing

The Arverne and Edgemere sectors of the peninsula are currently occupied by state and federal public housing, as well as residual small-scale duplex and single-family houses.

1 Arverne Houses, 1951: 410 units, fourteen six-story buildings (New York City Housing Authority, founded 1937)
2 Dayton Towers, 1971: cooperative apartments (Mitchell-Lama Housing, New York State, founded 1970)
3 Edgemere Houses, 1960s: 1,395 units (New York City Housing Authority, founded 1937)

In Arverne and Edgemere, most housing has fifty or more units per building, and the median income is approximately 22 percent of that in Queens; in fact, this sector of the Rockaway Peninsula has the third highest concentration of poverty in metropolitan New York. At the western end of the peninsula, affluent, predominantly Caucasian areas such as Neponsit and Belle Harbor are made up almost exclusively of single-family houses, and the average household income is 220 percent of the median income in Queens.

A combination of photographs and analytical diagrams can be used to describe the underpinnings of the territory and the quality of life there: residents of Arverne and Edgemere spend more of their income—and consequently more of their time—commuting to work than do the peninsula's wealthy Caucasian residents. A series of portraits by Caroline Dechaine reveal the quiet, isolated lives of public housing residents. A diagram shows the territory's legislative history and the major transformations effected by the 1937 Wagner-Steagall Act.

Stateless Architecture examined federal, state, and city policies, measuring them against alternate local and temporal means: the sky, the sea, the shifting sands, the ecologies. The new housing oscillates between these realms: Mark Rakatansky Studio produced housing influenced by the older slab buildings and vernacular houses. The Marble Fairbanks and Michael Bell projects integrated the infrastructure of street, sidewalk, and collective housing types with interwoven ground plans.

Housing Ecologies
Marble Fairbanks Architects
Target density: twenty-eight
units per acre
Average height: four stories

Stateless Housing
Michael Bell Architecture
Target density: eighteen
units per acre
Average height:
three stories

Urbia
Mark Rakatansky Studio
Target density: eight
units per acre
Average height: two stories

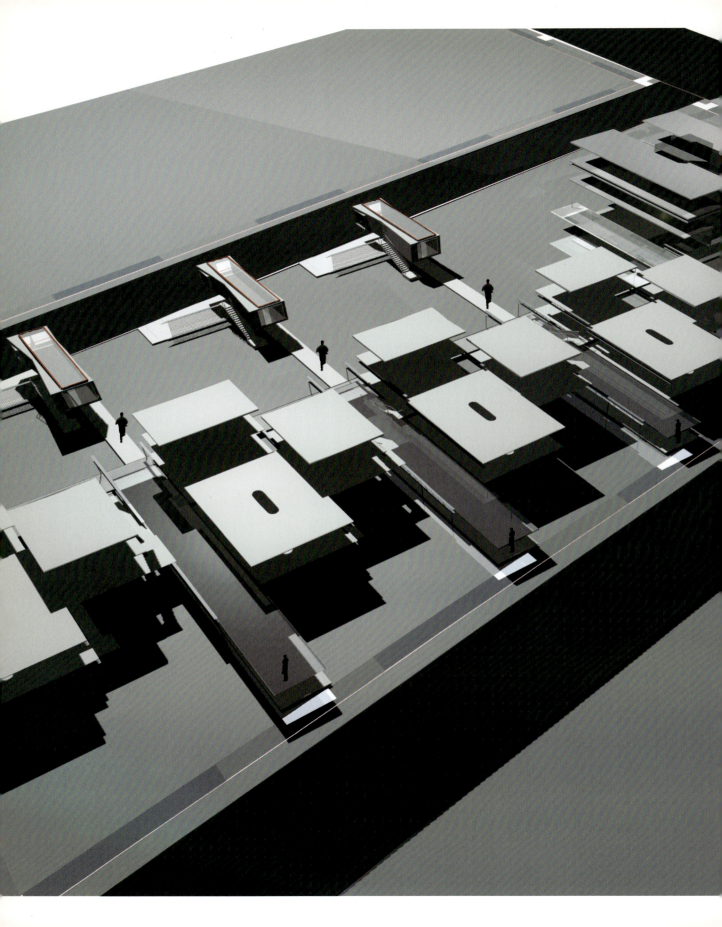

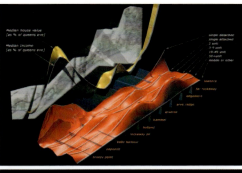

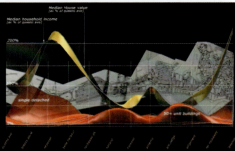

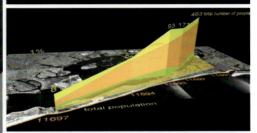

Percentage of average household income spent on travelling to work

Average Household Income / Number of Commuters

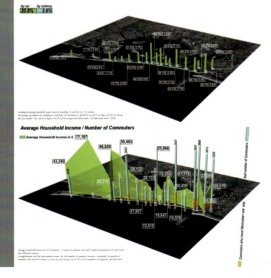

Prototypical Block: A New Figure-Ground; Not CIAM, Not New Urbanism

Stateless Housing was an attempt to define a new model of housing that combined the high-density, open-space paradigms of early modernism with the single-family house model common in the United States. The market tendency to subdivide property in order to build low-density, single-family units is here coupled with an attempt to promote density and collective housing types. The housing units are joined but individuated. The basic housing type employed is a triplex model—three units combined as a module. Each prototypical housing block contains four triplex modules and a higher-density duplex apartment building. The land underneath is left open so that natural vegetation can flourish.

In his essay "Aldo Rossi: The Idea of Architecture and the Modena Cemetery," Rafael Moneo parsed Rossi's writings to test the potential limits of Rossi's search for what he called the "specificity of the discipline of architecture," seeking the principles that Rossi argued allowed the city to be constructed and "produced from architecture."[1] Moneo was in some sense already wary of the degree to which this could be said to be true of the late modern city. He was aware that Rossi didn't necessarily associate building with physical construction; for Rossi, the construction of the city was not simply a matter of material production. In Moneo's appraisal, Rossi maintained an evasiveness about the role technology played in the construction of the contemporary city: "Rossi's architecture could be understood as an evasive one," he observed, "deliberately forgetting the framework of the real even at levels as evident and compromised as the technological one."

According to Moneo, this amnesia allowed Rossi to sustain a belief that architecture could indeed provide "urban facts" commensurate in their territorializing power with the forces of technology, communications, and capital that have long transcended cartographic borders and local territories. Moneo is an architect for whom building means either construction or the thought that accompanies building as occupation. In this context, architecture could still be said to construct the city, if it were considered a lens that enabled its inhabitants to reconstruct the city from a local vantage point. At Far Rockaway, this context becomes a touchstone, as the New York Department of Housing, Preservation, and Development has focused its attention on the construction of the city, the social and economic domains of poverty in which housing is located. The NYHPD's practical and logistical goals, however, focus on constructing housing. This dichotomy recalls the question Moneo asked of Rossi, testing architecture's limits as a social or political instrument in an era of more mobile and agile forms of urban spatial construction. Can housing solve the problems that Far Rockaway faces? The three architects who collaborated here to produce a new plan for Far Rockaway deployed architecture as a quasi-autonomous practice—each team designed housing—but at the core of the enterprise was an attempt to use housing to interpret the city.

Each team acknowledged the authority of the prevalent urban procedures—technology, politics, social, and economic realms—that many would argue have preconstructed Far Rockaway's relation to greater New York and the world. Here Moneo again provided a kind of touchstone: In describing the separation of working and dwelling spaces—the

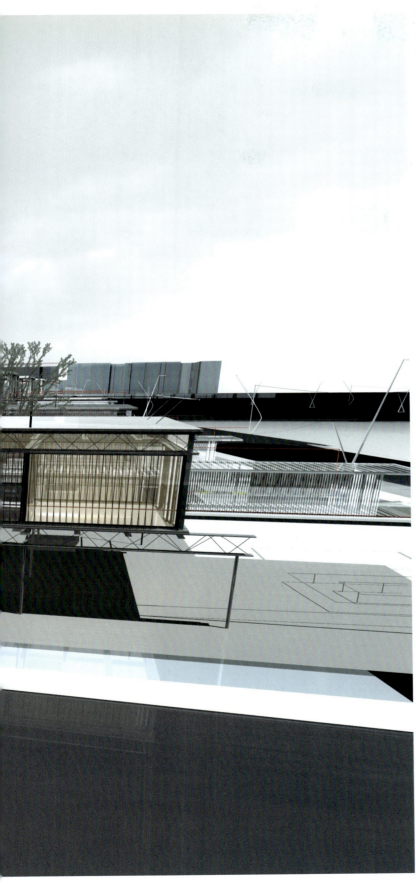

general condition of the modern city—he describes a scenario in which the problem of the city becomes that of the house. The house is a representation of the city; according to Rossi it is "a great representation of the human condition," the "fixed" scenery of architecture. Architecture offers a "glimpse" of the city, suspending local definitions of boundaries. Like Henri Bergson's description in *Matter and Memory* of a "movement-image" or a "time-image" as an intuited presence located "between a thing itself" and its representation,[2] architecture is here an intuiting device. In Far Rockaway, the goal has been to produce housing that offers the intuiting of space beyond the isolation of local borders. Architecture as time-image allows this remote site to remain fixed and defined by the borders of an RFP.

To borrow a phrase from Bergson, these three proposals "transcend space without stepping out from extensivity."[3] Each project in some sense blends the house and the city in a form that is intended to affirm the local as well as the broader metropolitan site. These works upset the autonomy of the political and economic systems that have played themselves out on the site and have had the subsequent effect of isolating the area from greater New York. These private houses are trying to form a city, and their urban significance lies in the degree to which they are believed to be capable of retaining the events of both the public and individual domains.[4] They offer an experience of the city from the inside of the house: to be in the house is to be in the city.

1 Rafael Moneo, "Aldo Rossi: The Idea of Architecture and the Modena Cemetery," *Oppositions* (Summer 1976): 4–9.
2 Henri Bergson, *Matter and Memory* (New York: Zone Books, 1988), 9–10.
3 Bergson, *Matter and Memory*, 179.
4 Moneo, "Aldo Rossi," 7.

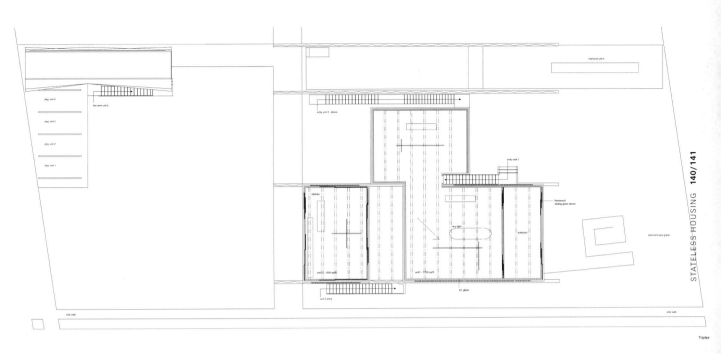

pkg. unit 4

pkg. unit 3

pkg. unit 2

pkg. unit 1

live work unit 5

live/work unit 4

entry unit 3 - above

entry unit 1

kitchen

fleetwood sliding glass doors

sky light

solarium

sand and sea grass

unit 3 - 1200 sqft

unit 1 - 1500 sqft

int. glass

unit 2 entry

side walk

side walk

Triplex

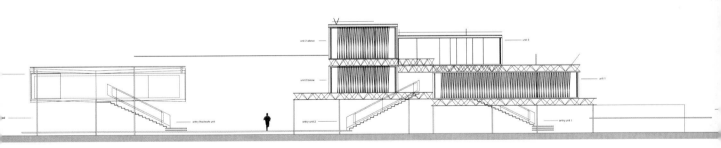

unit 2 above

unit 3

unit 2 below

unit 1

entry live/work unit

entry unit 2

entry unit 1

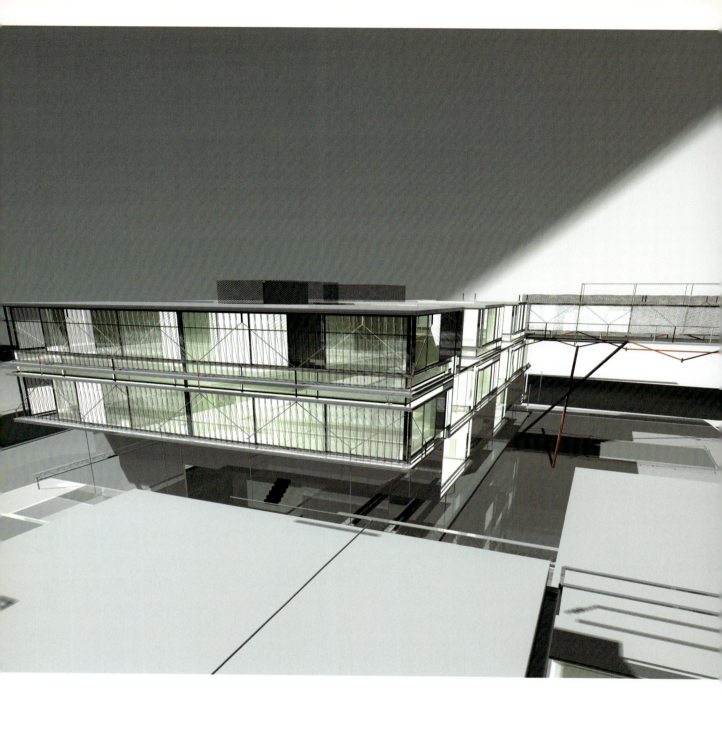

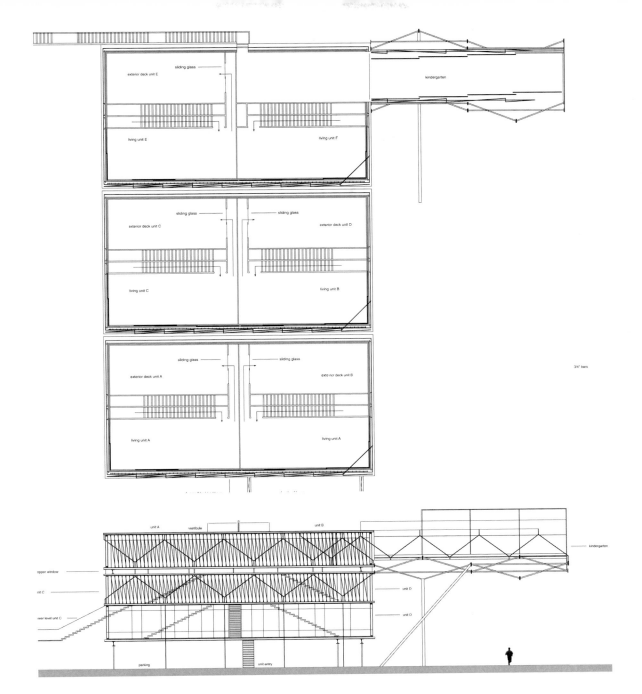

exterior deck unit E

sliding glass

living unit E

kindergarten

living unit F

sliding glass

sliding glass

exterior deck unit C

exterior deck unit D

living unit C

living unit B

3/4" bars

sliding glass

sliding glass

exterior deck unit A

exterior deck unit B

living unit A

living unit A

unit A

vestibule

unit B

kindergarten

upper window

unit D

nit C

unit D

lower level unit C

parking

unit entry

Station 1

Stations House

Client *Dwell* Magazine **Site** Pittsboro, North Carolina
Date of Design 2003 **Status** Designed

The Stations House was designed for a *Dwell* magazine competition for an affordable prefabricated house to be constructed on a site in North Carolina. From its inception, *Dwell* has made an attempt to introduce innovative housing to a mainstream shelter-magazine audience. While the magazine has not promoted a rigorous reintroduction of modernism in a formal, historical, or theoretical context, it has tried to offer an alternative to the neo-traditional housing that is prevalent in the United States.

The Stations House was designed to function practically and theoretically. It makes use of prefabricated components and high-end manufacturing techniques, but its major goal is to create a narrative of private life inside and around a highly commodified house. The building itself was influenced by the Catholic Stations of the Cross; each of the fourteen drawings interprets one of the stations as an interaction between house and occupant. The project is intended to draw attention to the dynamic tension between what the Werkbund termed "divine economies" and the Stations of the Cross as they show Christ becoming divine in death. The drawings juxtapose biblical narrative with architectural components and spaces, depicting a modern occupant living and moving through a highly technical, fabricated house. In the seemingly banal circumstances of everyday life, the house creates a tension between the body of the occupant and the material, or mechanical, body of the house. The goal was to reveal the common cleft between the deeply personal aspects of dwelling and the abstractions that highly evolved economic systems produce.

In this case, the theme of a divine and corporeal life that is transformed as it faces a societal power is taken to an extreme to reach a wide audience. As the stations progress, the body of the user slowly begins to merge with the structure of the house; in station thirteen, the body begins to deform and reorganize the house's structural system before it is removed from the house entirely in station fourteen. The drawings were created by altering the stability of tectonic structural systems with various artworks (painting and sculpture) that exhibit entropy and weight; the house slowly reveals a theme of bodily and material weight and a propensity to return material to the earth.

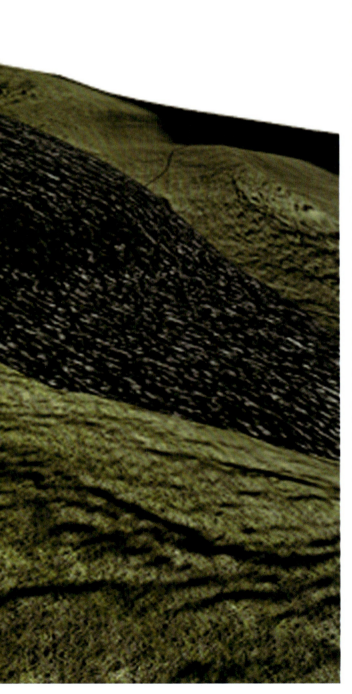

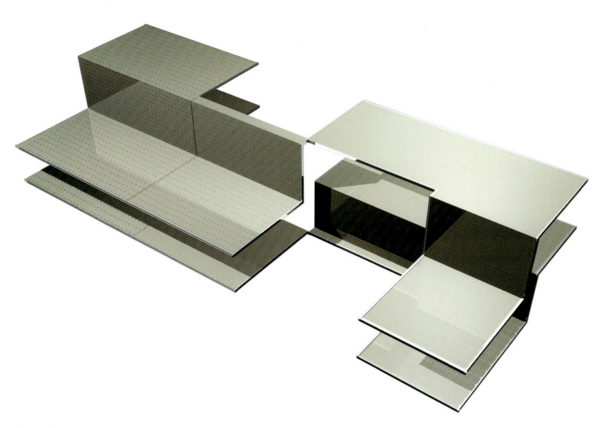

Station 2

Station 3

Station 4

Station 5

Station 6

Station 7

Station 8

Station 9

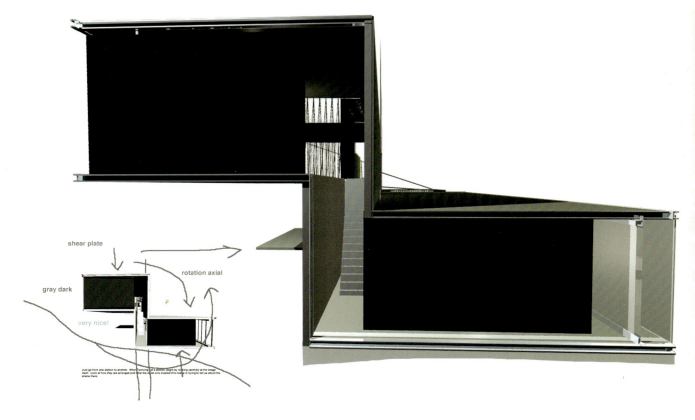

shear plate

gray dark

rotation axial

very nice!

Just go from one station to another. When entering of a station, begin by looking carefully at the image itself. Look at how they are arranged and what the artist who created this image is trying to tell us about the drama there.

Station 10

Station 11

Station 12

Station 13

Station 14

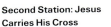
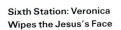
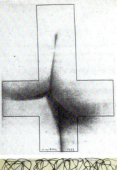

First Station: Jesus Is Condemned to Die

Entropy: Robert Smithson

Second Station: Jesus Carries His Cross

A stiff plate shell is self-supporting but only in certain directions. It opens itself volumetrically, refusing to provide closure. Giuseppe Terragni's work in statics and plate, or diaphragm, constructions: Palazzo Littorio, 1934. Plate construction pushed to the point of buckling.

Third Station: Jesus Falls the First Time

Despite the stillness, a collapse has occurred: we witness a man near us; we are one step removed, but within a range that allows empathy.

Push and pull as portrayed by Hans Hofmann in his painting *Ecstasy* were dynamic but ultimately balanced. Ray Eames, who studied with Hofmann, learned the forms of abstract expressionism from him. Her forms, like Hof-

mann's, were dynamic yet stable. The fall had yet to occur, although a collapse was built into the forms.

Fourth Station: Jesus Meets His Mother

Jesus's motion is simple, toward his mother in his suit and tie, as he does not realize it is he who is in need and he who faces danger—a simple rotation toward an empathic face. AEG, which has marketed household goods for a century, has now produced a house composed of woven surfaces that recalls the mass-produced Eames chair.

Fifth Station: Simon Helps Jesus Carry His Cross

A stair and a diagonal beam form a chord, spanning an arc; they provide still resolve to a tenuous system. Collapse is prevented, for the moment.

In Terragni's architecture, a balustrade can operate as a

beam; the stair is, in effect, a structural channel, rigid but tenuous.

Sixth Station: Veronica Wipes the Jesus's Face

Nivea Creme, ca. 1920: An imprint, a touch, comfort—but something more difficult and sorrowful as well. Our situation is reflected in the mirror, our otherness revealed in the most intimate acts.

Seventh Station: Jesus Falls the Second Time

He is seen through a layer of glass; he does not yet realize or accept his own destiny. A mural inscribed on the wall—on the plate of the house—shows a structural test. Failure is anticipated.

Eighth Station: Jesus Meets the Women of Jerusalem

Morris called the stripes of paint in his work "veils"; one can see through them to the canvas behind. Space itself is now draining, as energy

runs in small veins toward the earth.

Ninth Station: Jesus Falls the Third Time

On the third fall, he is seen from inside the house, across the courtyard. Witnessed from a distance, he is two layers removed.

Tenth Station: Jesus Is Stripped

Glass is painted black in a manner that recalls the *Stations of the Cross* (1958–66) by Barnett Newman. A line is drawn and a negative space opens in the flatness of the plane.

Eleventh Station: Jesus Is Nailed to the Cross

A panoramic view allows the horizon to curve: we are cast into space, and the stability of time is eradicated as the station point fails.

Twelfth Station: Jesus Dies on the Cross

Becoming divine, not human.

Thirteenth Station: Jesus Is Taken Down from the Cross

The arcing fall of the body in the Pietà is projected into the network and negative spaces of Brice Marden's *Cold Mountain* paintings (1988–91). The body deforms the void, unwinding the house's walls: space prevails as time and production fail to become divine.

Fourteenth Station: Jesus Is Laid in the Tomb

After the cantilever and the attempt to open space while allowing for production, we leave the scene of architecture and return to nature, moving on to new forms of immanent life.

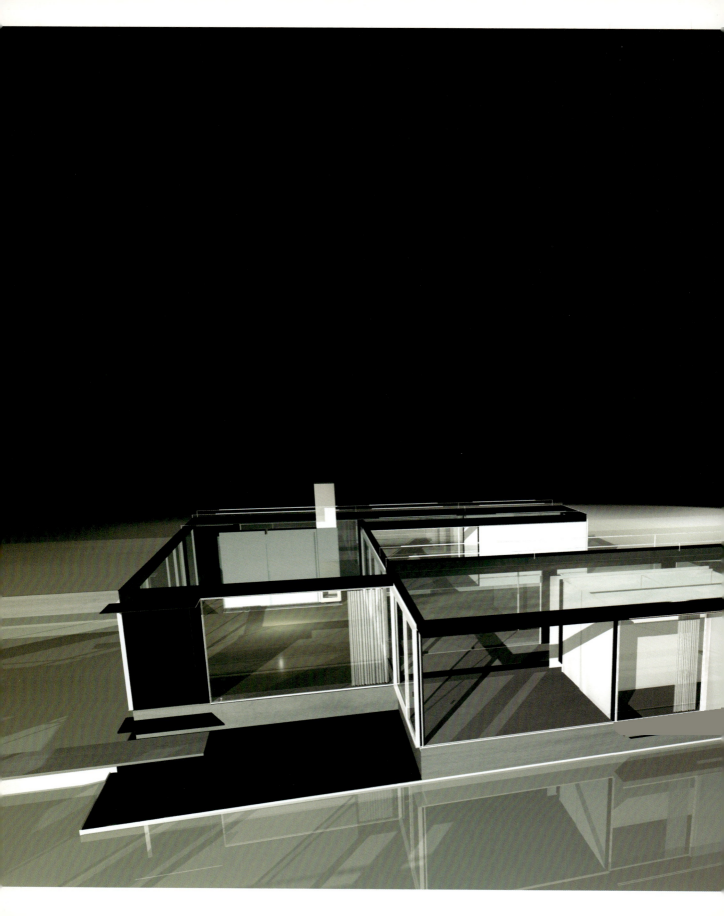

Binocular House

Client Philip Gefter and Richard Press **Site** Ghent, New York
Date of Design 2003 **Status** Under Construction

The Binocular House is located on a wooded, twelve-acre site surrounded by an eight-hundred-acre farm in Ghent, New York; the right-of-way to the densely forested site cuts across an open field. One hundred seventeen miles north of midtown Manhattan in Columbia County, Ghent has become the most recent extension of the New York arts community with the opening of the Dia Beacon and the presence of many other arts organizations as well.

The house's owners—*New York Times* page-one photo editor Philip Gefter and filmmaker Richard Press—live and work in Manhattan. The 2,280-square-foot, two-bedroom Binocular House, which includes two studies for writing, was designed to serve their photographic interests and, conceptually, to develop themes that emerged in other projects, such as the Stations House. The building uses a geothermal heating and cooling system and high-performance glass to keep its energy consumption on par with that of a traditional house. A series of planar glass walls—all double-glazed and argon-filled—layer space from west to east. In two places, the layers allows the gaze to pass through the house to the forest beyond; the deep background is shown on the glazed facade of the house.

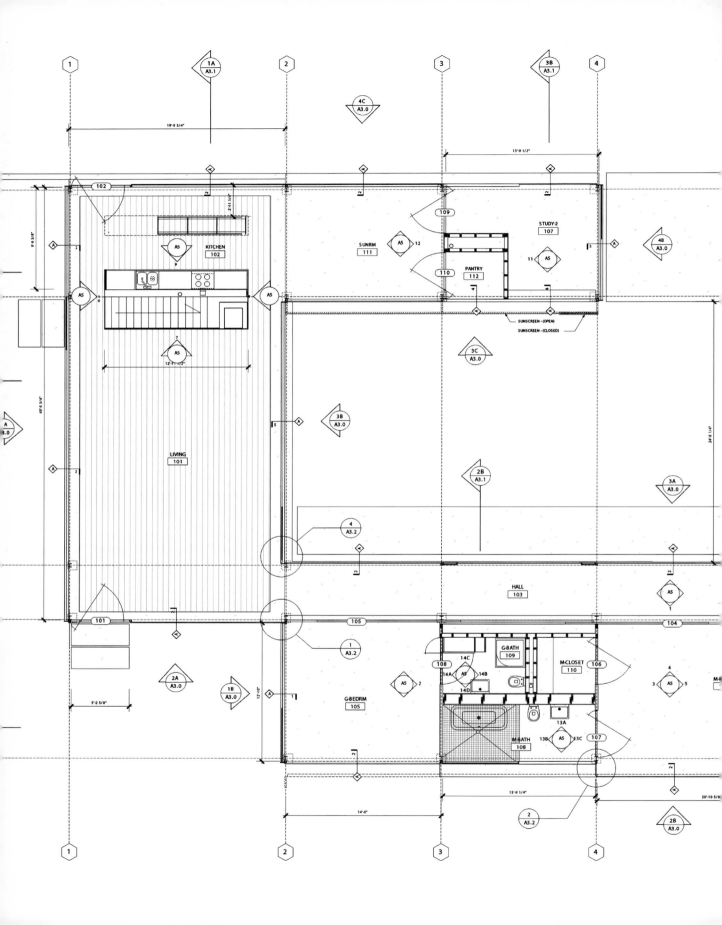

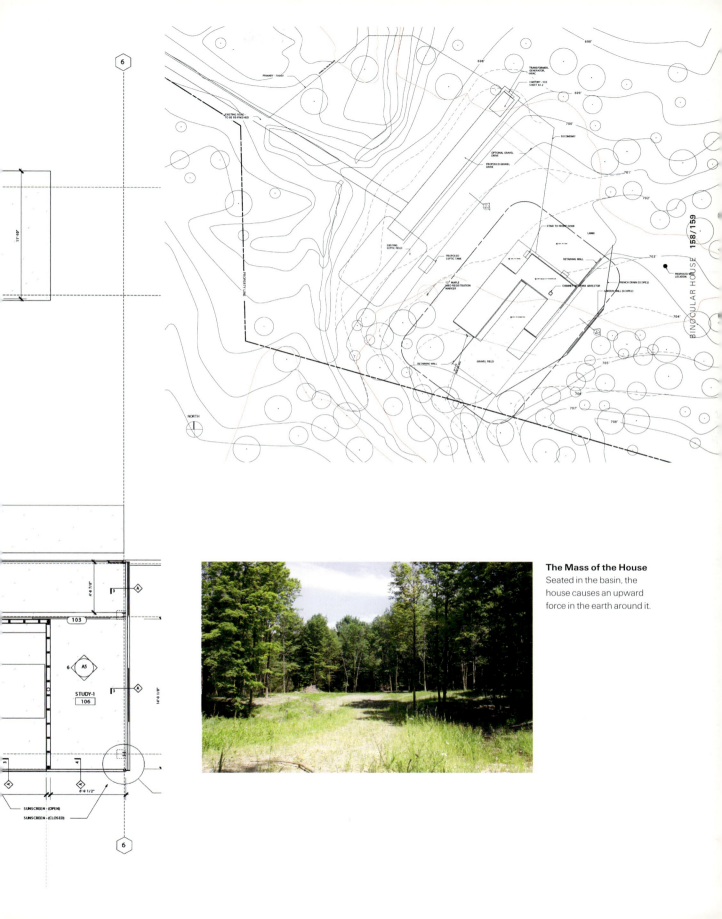

NORTH

The Mass of the House
Seated in the basin, the house causes an upward force in the earth around it.

FIG 1 Mitchell-Lama Housing, Arverne, Far Rockaway, New York

Introduction

Arverne and Edgemere, two adjacent neighborhoods on the Far Rockaway Peninsula in Queens, New York, have the highest concentration of poverty in the city. They also contain the largest developable tract of land in metropolitan New York. An unplanned natural habitat situated between Jamaica Bay and the Atlantic Ocean on an otherwise extremely dense outer edge of the city, the property comprises more than three hundred acres left vacant after the monumental slum-clearing acts of modern urban renewal in the late 1960s.

The land was never redeveloped despite a critical need for affordable housing and at least four highly publicized proposals for as many as ten thousand units of low-income housing. The last significant development on the peninsula was the public housing that defines the current borders of the cleared land, built between the 1940s and 1970s on Edgemere's bay and south of the Beach 67th Street elevated subway station in Arverne, once a flourishing site of early twentieth-century bungalows and resort hotels. Until recently, the political will and the essential capital to rebuild were eclipsed by ideological battles about what and for whom to build. No reciprocal means of rebuilding at a scale commensurate with the monolithic clearing has surfaced since the 1960s—nothing has assured the regeneration of the site at either a public or private level.

A barrier island, the Rockaway Peninsula is a delicate ecosystem wracked by a culture of poverty unique even to United States federal housing. The site's original tidal land formation is a hybrid of the rural and the metropolitan. Sited at the final stop of the A train, the peninsula is part of metropolitan New York, but the presence of Jamaica Bay and the vacant expanses of city property, as well as the long commute to Manhattan, make it a rural outpost.

The sublime vacuousness of this oceanfront land belies how circumscribed life at the outpost actually is. The apparently pastoral quality of the land and its relationship to the bay and the ocean are at odds with the homogeneity of the racial organization in the New York City Housing Authority's developments and the residents' lack of social and economic mobility. To a large degree, the vacant space on the Rockaway Peninsula has also helped sustain the adjacent public housing's sense of isolation and anomie. The housing creates a highly constructed territory that stands in apparent opposition to the surrounding open terrain. An anomaly in New York, this area's potential for reconstruction speaks not only to the future of the city, but to the way we conceive urban space in the United States as a whole.

The land is owned by the New York Department of Housing, Preservation and Development, which was founded in 1971 and has served as a receivership for properties since the city's near bankruptcy in the mid-1970s. Based on a model of planned obsolescence, the HPD returns city holdings to the market at lowered valuations to create a financial incentive for redevelopment; the agency will cease to exist after its land and housing assets have been redistributed to public-private redevelopment partnerships.

At Arverne and Edgemere, where three eras of public housing form the borders of the HPD property, the agency is now subsidizing new market-rate housing intended to attract residents with a much higher income level, in an effort to reduce the concentration of low-income tenants in the area. Unlike the adjacent public housing, however, this new quasi-market-rate housing will not reveal its subsidies: the HPD, whose goal is to diminish the outward signs of its assistance, has donated the property to a developer, so that the housing will, in effect, appear to have been built without the support of the state. Rockaway, a zone of last resort for a racially and economically homogeneous population living below the poverty line, will be transformed by new quasi-traditional housing and a new quasi-traditional urbanism.

LIVING AND WORKING

In describing the separation of dwelling and working spaces characteristic of the modern city, Rafael Moneo depicted a scenario in which the problem of the city becomes one of housing. At Arverne and Edgemere the problem of housing is indeed the problem of the city. The urban condition is likewise a domestic one as people try to navigate the inchoate fabric and expansive emptiness of this remote but still urban area. In the absence of better transportation, higher paying jobs, or full-scale urban redevelopment, a new architecture must embrace the history of both the public and private domains—from the state processes that have constructed prior housing milieus to the market guise development now takes—addressing aspects of power that are beyond its local province.

The Rockaway Peninsula provided a point of departure for each of the following three chapters—Stateless Spaces I, II, and III. The overarching theme is one of empathy, not in the sense of the word's popular connotation, but instead as a means of exploring difference and otherness as inevitable consequences of late twentieth-century modernization. At Arverne and Edgemere—and, indeed, in much of the United States—urban and domestic space have been routinely characterized as highly instrumental, yet also vacuous, if not drained of plastic and private content. Complete territories have been literally removed—cleared away—leaving emptied spaces in the urban landscape. No one believes these vacancies truly represent a sublime site of freedom, yet they have become a place of intellectual and practical exchange, providing an impetus for architects to renew their relationship with political science and a wide range of social and technical concerns. The result is far from conclusive, and in many ways this lack of conclusiveness can be seen as sustaining the existing fragmentation. Rife with personal struggle and injustice, these sites encourage an urbanism where injustice would ideally be addressed; in the absence of such a provision, however, it falls to the occupant to find new means of understanding the realms of power beyond his control.

Stateless Spaces I

1990S LOS ANGELES: CITY OF REFUGEES

In the early 1990s, two books were widely discussed in architectural circles for their prescient attempts to examine what was commonly known as the "contemporary city," a term used in the 1990s to describe a city of immense potential that was also distressed and fragmented by its own self-sustaining processes. Both Mike Davis's *City of Quartz: Excavating the Future in Los Angeles*[1] and André Corboz's *Looking for a City in America*[2] focused on Los Angeles, the site of the widespread rioting that followed the announcement of the Rodney King verdict in 1992, and both could be said to view the city—the contemporary city—as a place where it was common to feel

1 Mike Davis, *City of Quartz: Excavating the Future in Los Angeles* (New York: Vintage Books, 1992).
2 André Corboz, *Looking for a City in America: Down These Mean Streets a Man Must Go: An Essay by André Corboz* (Santa Monica: Getty Center for the History of Art and the Humanities, 1992).

FIG 2 Residents of
Ocean Village, New York

like, if not actually be, a refugee. Mike Davis and André Corboz were predisposed to examining class struggles and economic inequity in Marxist terms, and to a certain melancholy in the way they viewed the empty promise of the city. The books gained wide influence and can be credited with helping to renew an architectural and urban planning conversation based on geography and race, as well as the strife that was vivid and palpable in the Los Angeles of the time.

Davis's book was, in its literal form, a kind of urban history, but it also relied on a noirish fiction to convey its history of Los Angeles's growth and metamorphosis. While its narrative descriptions of power plays and racial districting in Los Angles were compelling—and, to a large extent, historically accurate—what gave the book lasting value was the way it opened the door to a new relationship with Los Angeles and, more important, to the latter-day United States city itself. *City of Quartz* helped reinvent the city as a subject for a new generation of architects and urban theorists who were no longer working on the historic city, but instead on understanding our time and place, without having yet acquired the conceptual tools to move forward meaningfully.

Davis analyzed the underpinnings of political and economic power in Los Angeles, but he also examined the literal geography and growth of the city. Locating his scenarios with literal street signs and within districts and neighborhoods, he depicted the power plays between politicians, labor unions, and workers. Davis's narrative oscillated between politics and physical place, creating a tension that, in effect, called into question the degree to which power failed to be fully revealed in the physical geometry and organization of the contemporary city. In all of his cultural and economic sketches of Los Angeles, however, he never directly discussed architecture except in a short chapter titled "Frank Gehry as Dirty Harry," in which he accused the architect of turning his back on the city with the inward facing, insular new Goldwyn Public Library in Hollywood. Davis may have misunderstood the complexity of Gehry's inside-out building, but his writing fascinated architects whose work was enabled by a new sense of purpose, despite being thwarted by forces beyond its professional and spatial reach.

Davis left architecture's role in the city in a disaffected condition, reaching for authority but increasingly circumscribed by more nimble power and procedural means. Troubled by its own lack of agency, architecture became a local site from which to reconstruct urban space as well as urban subjectivity. Of course, one could look to other writers to describe this same scenario—architectural agency has been commonly depicted as eclipsed by urban finance and economic procedures—yet Davis's sense of urgency incited architects to respond anew. Architecture's formal histories—its plastic histories—were in crisis, but if the contemporary city could be newly imagined, so too could contemporary architecture. Davis's message—that the city's power structures were dangerously predatory precisely because they were not revealed—invoked an architecture that needed to carry the burden of literal place and to give presence to the underlying network of private interests that constructed the city.

LOOKING FOR A CITY IN AMERICA

André Corboz's book was more conventionally architectural and essentially urban in its presentation of property divisions and the mathematics and geometry of urban form. Yet his subtitle, "Down These Mean Streets a Man Must Go," made him Davis's partner in both the melancholy and the existential drafting of the city. Unlike Davis, however, Corboz focused on the city's syntax: in contraposition to Robert Venturi, Denise Scott Brown, and Steven Izenour's *Learning from Las Vegas* and Colin Rowe and Fred Koetter's *Collage City*, Corboz characterized Mario Gandelsonas's *The Order of the American City* as creating a "firm groundwork for an analysis of American urban morphology," a sympathetic reading of a theory based in a figure-ground mapping of American cities. *Learning from Las Vegas* was, in Corboz's words, based in the "epiphenomena" of media and advertising, and *Collage City* verged on "Dadaist irresponsibility." Corboz, like Davis, was not so much seeking to determine a new theory of urban formal syntax (even as he applauded Gandelsonas's work), but to address a social and political crisis within a city that despite its "monotonous" and "undifferentiated" qualities was also being effaced and was, for many, devoid social or economic opportunity. Corboz's city, at its worst, "warehouses" human beings. His analysis sought to project the city in formal and political historical structures. His urban subject was reliant on the primacy and literalness of physical form, but he was also aware that it was the policies and economies beneath these forms that needed to be addressed.

Why then seek form at all? What means does it hold? The American city, according to Corboz, was always intended to remain undifferentiated, and in some sense unanchored, to a historic city center. It was "physiocratically" derived from a deep opposition to a monarchial capital city, writes Corboz, who relies on Thomas Jefferson's Land Ordinance of 1785 as the originative syntactic grid that stabilized the American plains but also sustained their perpetual extension and subdivision. The open-ended grid of the American continent dissipates the center city into a continual, enveloping, endless landscape that, in its present-day urban form, has ceased to provide the intended escape from centralized power: instead it represents a vacuum of social entropy and monotony.

RACE

In his introduction to *Looking for a City in America*, Kurt Forster offered a view of the city and the social and political realm that augmented Corboz's inquiry. The vantage of Forster's essay was to a large degree derived from an awareness of racial inequality, as was Davis's work. "The physically compact historic city," wrote Forster, "has long been considered the crucible where the alchemy of new multiracial and multicultural life could take hold; but the reality of inner-city conditions in the United States has rarely been able to sustain these hopes." When the two books were released, it was clear that racial relations were not being sustained by either the edge city— the sprawling city—or the dense historic center city such as New York. The most significant question, however, was implied, if not asked directly: to what degree, if at all, did the physical form of the contemporary city play a role in the social or political relations between its constituents?

Looking for a City in America was published by the Getty Center, which at the time was attempting to establish its own legitimacy in racial and class relations in Los Angeles. The Getty must have published Corboz's book as part of its mission to address the cultural scenarios embedded in its own art historicism and the multiracial complexity of its host city, in an effort to dissimulate the citadel-like quality of its own urban design and the monolithic aspect of its financial power. Its mission entailed a search for a new city, an alternative understanding of urbanism that could sustain the development of Los Angeles without necessitating the dense urbanism of New York City or the protohistoric form of the then-burgeoning New Urbanism. If it was possible for Corboz and Davis to reinhabit the dissipative spaces of Los Angeles and other sprawling cities, then such an alternative new city might be possible.

AMERICAN TERRAIN VAGUE

Forster's introduction to Corboz's book was just two pages long, but it captivated an audience of emerging urban theorists who, like Corboz, were beginning to test the limits of another key term in recent urban theory, *terrain vague*. The phrase had been popularized in Europe through the writings of Manuel de Solá-Morales. In Solá-Morales's use of the term, it described—or quite purposefully failed to describe—a panoramic yet disjointed perspective that gained breadth, but lost coherence, as it approached the periphery of buildings. Terrain vague described architecture's inability to give coherence to the chasms, vacancies, and gaps that abound in the contemporary city. The implication of Solá-Morales's argument was that the mass and literal presence of buildings—of architecture—mattered little in the formation of the contemporary urban landscape, and therefore architectural practice needed to come to terms with a role that was spatially and economically marginal. Negative space was predominant in contemporary urbanism in many new European edge cities. Terrain vague represented a conceptual as well as literal challenge for architects: it called attention to the spaces adjacent to architecture—not only outside our conceptual discourse, but outside our professional realm as well—and in its essential logic it challenged architects to seek to cohere spaces that were beyond the boundaries of their practices.

Forster's introduction gave legitimacy to a North American version of terrain vague. *Looking for a City in America* was in part a reconnaissance mission charged with defining the urban ground upon which the Getty was locating itself, addressing an array of urban theorists who sought an alternative to a renewed interest in historic city form. In the wake of the Los Angeles riots, Corboz and Forster were understood as presenting a new view of the distended geography of the American postwar city, and the veracity of the book's publisher offered intellectual venture capital to a tentative group of younger theorists who saw links between European ideas of a terrain vague and edge cities in the United States such as Phoenix, Houston, Los Angeles, and Atlanta. The book's designer, Bruce Mau, later collaborated with Rem Koolhaas on *SMLXL*, which at its core addressed similar conditions worldwide. With Mau's characteristic full-page bleeds and rhythmic pacing, *Looking for a City in America* evoked the expansive blankness of the city it addressed and, in effect, began a process of revealing the sublime beauty of Los Angeles's fragmented space. Davis and Corboz both portrayed their urban subjects against this emptied space, navigating a territory whose dimensions vacillated between a literal cartography of lot sizes and property lines and the otherwise invisible properties of power that delaminate these physical forms.

In New York, the idea of terrain vague would at first seem less relevant than it does in a national context, yet in 2001 the city began a long-range project of rezoning sectors of all five boroughs in order to affirm its historic urban density. The rezoning is intended to make sure New York City remains competitive with surrounding regional alternatives for both commercial and housing uses. Areas of the city that were subject to violence during the height of the 1960s civil

3 William Faulkner, *Light in August* (New York: Vintage International Edition, Random House, 1990), 8.
4 Robert A. Caro, *The Power Broker: Robert Moses and the Fall of New York* (New York: Vintage Books, 1975), 611.

rights strife are again sites of re-urbanization. New racial and economic identities are being established as the city attempts to shore up its foundations as host to the world's financial institutions and as a center of global culture.

Stateless Spaces II
EMPATHY: SOUTHERN TIME—NORTHERN POLICIES

"After a while she began to hear the wagon . . . the sound of it seems to come slow and terrific and without meaning, as though it were a ghost traveling a half mile ahead of its own shape. 'That far within my hearing before my seeing,' Lena thinks." [3]

In William Faulkner's novel *Light in August*, first published in 1932, the writer's descriptions of the languid, heat-soaked mill towns of the South are matched by those of a character whose identity was sustained in a simultaneous affirmation and rejection of the limitations of her current situation. Faulkner's protagonist, Lena, occupies events before and after they occur: "That far within my hearing before my seeing," she says to herself as the wagon that is to carry her into her future breaches the envelope of space she occupies as it emerges over the hill. Spatial dimensions are affirmed and simultaneously made relative by segregating the senses—the local position is recast into a field traced by the newly extensive limits of past and future circumstance. Lena overcomes the isolation of her circumstances by perceptual means.

The years immediately following the publication of *Light in August* saw the advent of the New Deal legislation that provided the first federal subsidies for low-income housing in the United States. Together, the National Housing Act of 1934 and the Wagner-Steagall Act of 1937 allocated $800 million in the form of federal loans to states to develop housing for those who had fallen by the wayside of the market economy.[4] The funding was predominantly destined for the industrial and urban North, and in New York City the inordinate prospect of $300 million made the newly formed Housing Authority an epicenter of urban design and development. From that point on, housing policy influenced architectural and urban design, as well as racial and economic identity. Modern architecture, a tool of the Federal Housing Authority, accommodated new policies that were decried by many as quasi-socialist and antimarket. In his introduction to *Five Architects*, however, Colin Rowe repudiated this charge and condemned American modernism for being, in fact, devoid of clear "political pedigree." Only at its physical and temporal origins in Europe, he contended, was modern architecture an adjunct of socialism, ideologically rooted in Marxism. Rowe's assertion about American modernism, though resoundingly clear at the time of publication in 1975, was inconclusive when it came to understanding American public housing completed under the auspices of modern planning. Rowe's derision still resonates, however, and one wonders if public housing in the United States was ever ideologically modern at all, even if its prewar forms appeared to be so. The racial and economic homogeneity of its demographics meant that public housing was a refuge of last resort from capitalism, as well as a way of racially and economically stratifying the population.

In Vienna, the Karl Marx Hof was completed in 1930, a couple of years prior to the publication of Faulkner's novel and almost a full decade before the New York City Housing Authority was founded. But the Social Democratic Workers' Party, weakened beyond effectiveness, left the completed building as a signifier of the absent Socialist goals that sustained its political character and its public and private programming. Robert Musil's *The Man Without Qualities* was published in Vienna in 1932, virtually concurrent with Faulkner's work; it too unfolds through the spatial and temporal intuition of a character whose relationship to the world is essentially one of alienation. Both Faulkner and Musil offer their subjects as passengers rather than moderators of time and space. For Faulkner, the site was the American South; for Musil, it was an emergent twentieth-century European metropolis. Both portray characters who are possessed and entrapped by local circumstance and time; even as the body is presented as the locus of knowledge, the characters' comprehension of circumstance is shown to be inadequate to sustain their own fragmented identities.

Musil's central character, Ulrich, seems to fall out of the whole choreography of metropolitan time and into a chasm whose emptiness leaves him searching for his own essence. Ulrich is "two separate people, one of whom" lives according to "serene rules in a world where reality did not exist."[5] Ulrich's emotions have been prewritten and pre-experienced, foreclosing on the veracity of the immediate, forcing him to disregard his own senses. Because of the over-construction of his identity, he finds himself alienated from his own position in space and his own body. Musil and Faulkner both insist on material and immediate conditions as the touchstone of knowledge, but they reject any practices that attempt to derive self-knowledge from that finite field. They verify the early modern subject's presence—and even nullify the power of the commodity procedures or social loss that enforce their alienation—through a highly quantified physicality, yet they also perhaps tragically leave the subjects on their own, as stilled signifiers of an absent social, political, or economic process that might sustain sovereign identity. Although the linearity of their narratives and the sequential nature of time they inhabit produces a sense of weight and potential energy, it is also what victimizes them. The tension between the linearity of what they can see and what they only sense, between the knowledge of the present and the yet-to-be-lived future, creates an immanent force that, if revealed, could extend the otherwise foreclosed aspects of time that determine their fortunes.

Stateless Spaces III

JOHN HEJDUK'S FORM-PROGRAMS: NO CITY

With the creation of the Berlin Masque in 1981, John Hejduk moved from making individual works of architecture to inventing ensembles of buildings grouped under the rubric "masques." The buildings were titled according to their proposed locations—the Berlin Masque, the Lancaster/Hanover Masque—and were designed in succession until 1992. Although each was planned for a different site, the essential structure of the masques remained the same. The identity of the host city or territory was acknowledged, but not through urban form or geographic particularity. Instead, the masques took up residence in their host cities as encampments, temporary ensembles of buildings and subjects. Hejduk's urbanism was temporal, and it was based on identifying his subjects as much as it was on identifying building forms. Each building was designed for a specific occupant and defined by a narrow program. In each case, a larger sense of

5 Robert Musil, *The Man Without Qualities*, trans. Eithne Wilkins and Ernst Kaiser (London: Picador, 1979), 34.

6 John Hejduk, "Out of Time and Into Space," in *Mask of Medusa: Works 1947–1983*, ed. Kim Shkapich (New York: Rizzoli International Publications, 1985), 71–75.

program was left undeveloped. Within the Berlin Masque, for example, one could find the House for the Mother of the Suicide and the House for the Masque Taker, and while each was indeed a house, it was the connection between subject and form that sustained the creative work.

Hejduk's buildings always carefully fabricated their own contexts—his work was done in series or multiples—but their meaning was derived from historical context as well. His early accomplishments were influenced, in particular, by the work of Mies van der Rohe. In his seminal Texas Houses, Hejduk began a project of designing in multiples; each of the seven houses was created by testing the limits of the house that preceded it. Later, Hejduk's work followed a thread found in that of Le Corbusier; with his Wall Houses, he began a prolonged investigation of cubism and a kind of postcubist stillness, which he illuminated in his essay "Out of Time and Into Space."[6] In it, Hejduk analyzed Le Corbusier's Carpenter Center using a paradigm of cubist spatial techniques and concluded with the assertion that a potential new architectural space would emerge if "the tension and compression, the push-pull" common to the viscous work of cubism that sustained Corbusier's first investigations was exceeded. This viscous space, he observed, "may have therapeutic value to the docile; the question remains, at what point do the harmonic fluctuations crack causing dissolution and failure of the spatial organism?"

Hejduk's work is generally considered to have maintained a cubist quality of thickened space, but his compositions are better understood as postcubist. The plan of the Bye House, for example, is explained by focusing on the hypotenuse as a threshold moment, a flattening of space that places the building's biomorphic forms against a planar background. The rendering of the Bye House gives another reading: the biomorphic forms do indeed take shape against the background wall, but they are drawn as negative forms, extractions from space. They have become semi-negative, yet they remain plastic, traced and defined by a chiaroscuro, a thickening of atmosphere at their edges. The trees, the site, and the literally organic and biomorphic forms of nature are given predominance in the drawing.

While the rendering can be described as a cubist composition—a still life against a neutralized plane—studying the periphery and the surreal drawing of the trees and landscape reveals that it is more than that. The transformation that set the stage for the masque, refocusing our attention from a single building to an expanded field of nature and site, is evident. This transformation, which simultaneously placed the individual within a singular and identifiable work, created a still life within a wider space.

Hejduk's composition and its intended subjects (the occupants of the various houses) exhibit the same stillness and narrative that Picasso showed in the early 1920s, in a painting of a harlequin done after his cubist period. A linearity and a sequential nature of time are present in this painting (*Portrait of Jacinto Salvado as Harlequin*, 1923)—as they are in another, similar painting of a harlequin produced in 1918 (*Harlequin with Violin*), during his cubist period—yet in the stillness of the postcubist work one senses a potential energy, an immanent force. The character appears in front of the picture plane, and its role is defined as segregate but within a wider field, as in a masque.

The masque reaffirms the interiority of each architectural work, showing us a city of atomized lives, isolated interiors, and private stillness, but it reorients our comprehension of space to incorporate a wider incipient urban field as well. Hejduk's Bye House can be understood to curtail the interiority of the house; it is not only an agent of privacy and repose, but also a device that makes the inhabitant other to a city constructed by histories of fiscal and governmental policy. Hejduk's architecture transcends what he calls the "harmonic fluctuations" of plastic space, and in doing so it gives retroactive coherence to the dissolution of space in the wider field, the urban or natural field.

The Wall Houses suggest an evolutionary understanding of an unframed space and an unframed city. In other words, if architecture can turn itself inside out and, in effect, cast the subject into a wider landscape whose attributes are voided, the masque reflects the metaphysical project in which the locus of time is discovered to be within each character. That is, time is within in each person and within the collective assembly of persons and materials: everyone is an origin—and everyone is other.

AT ARVERNE

In 1997, several years before I became involved in proposing new housing for Arverne and Edgemere as part of a research project for the HPD, I founded a similar program in Houston. As part of that project, I commissioned a photographer named Deron Neblett to document life in Houston's Fifth Ward. During my work on the Rockaway Peninsula, I found myself returning to those pictures, comparing them to a set of portraits done by Caroline Dechaine in Arverne, and the John Hejduk masques came to mind.

In Houston, the proposal was for sixteen houses scattered throughout the Fifth Ward; in Far Rockaway, it was for eighteen hundred units of new housing on a hundred cleared acres. But in both cases, it was the images and the stillness of the residents that stood out. Three of the original eighty images from Houston, in particular, seemed to resonate: a small girl sitting on a metal chair, a man in a church pew, and a young entrepreneur using a computer in a ramshackle house. They recalled two of the photos from New York, one of a young girl reading in the courtyard of Ocean Village, another of a woman pulling open the drapes in her apartment. In each case, I found myself returning to the singularity of their actions and the isolation in which they occurred. Their *otherness* in relation to the very rooms and surfaces of their lives demanded a closer look and a new understanding: the vinyl and the bent tubing of the young girl's chair, the paneling in the room where the man worked on his computer. When I began my work in this neighborhood where the average household income was $7,800 a year, I felt at a loss to describe the poverty. These images made it real, but they revealed a quiet repose as well. The portraits of the Fifth Ward reflected life in the midst of self-regulating urban systems; the cruel effects of poverty were obvious in terms of health, education, and safety, and yet I found myself looking for a new way to describe the poverty that would acknowledge the kind of sanctuary in which these individuals resided.

I think the masque works this way, and one could find value for contemporary urbanism in its embodiment of the transitory within the still. Hejduk was drawing our lives, and the only way he knew to give presence to them was by delineating the outside. Certainly a sense of melancholy (if not, at times, despair) can be found in his work, but there is also the sense of a subject whose agency and sovereignty is made explicit but nevertheless seen as terribly precarious.

FIG 3 Resident of Fifth Ward, Houston, Texas

In Far Rockaway, the inchoate yet power-laden spaces of contemporary urbanism can be reread through Hejduk's lens. Sanctuary is provided not by the architectural forms, but by the sovereignty they offer their subjects. That this sovereignty is afforded in the turning of space inside out—in the casting of subject into space and, as Hejduk would have it, "out of time"—is both harrowing and thrilling. What kind of dynamics are possible for new architectural space in the latter-day modern city—the contemporary city whose centers are decimated by relentless redevelopment and expansive new edge cities? What new subjects—and new programs—can we imagine within these new spaces? And what agency could assure the survival of these new subjects and programs within and without the former metropolis?

As world governments increasingly attempt to create and shore up urban and suburban straits between zones occupied by competing financial interests, space becomes literally stateless, and as it is emptied of the final strains of a Marxist critique based on an equitable distribution of assets, its vacancies become zones of sublime statelessness where subjects navigate empty spaces. Here there is the potential for a new kind of urban occupant, and perhaps a new architecture, but the relevance of such an architecture will come only if it is accompanied by a deep respect for the lives that have sustained these stilled zones, which we have mistakenly understood as devoid of potential.

In Max Weber's *The Protestant Ethic and the Spirit of Capitalism*, religious feeling and action serve as the agar in which human beings fashion themselves in greatest possible complicity with their social and economic worlds. The astonishing confluence of economics and religion as prime, and complementary, motors of human subjectivity, even in modernity (the very definition of modernity itself?), is almost as surprising today as it was before the work of the great economic historians of the latter half of the nineteenth century. There is once again a great deal of talk about a "human subject," although very little of significance or depth is getting said. Perhaps this is because the "subject" was never meant to be a psychological category, but rather an *effect* of how matter is organized, how it is set into motion, how it becomes action.

One need not be a Weberian, or even a Marxist, to be a materialist in this manner. Every architect, in fact, whether he or she knows and admits it or not, is such a materialist, either failed or successful. We know this thanks to practices like Michael Bell's. From his earliest essay-projects such as House Inside Out, through the powerfully city-committed "Eyes in the Heat," to *Space Replaces Us*, Bell's work speaks with an almost Augustinian tone of the world in which humans take form as one revealed in geometries and forces. But like both Leonardo and Darwin before him, Bell understands that the function always creates the organ. A subject is taking shape everywhere, and it has nothing to do with us. In Bell's revealed world, space represents the godlike force that invests, inhabits, or, to use the ancient phrase, *participates* in worldly being by endowing matter with temporal qualities (thus ours is always a *Slow Space*). Everything good and ill flows from this ceaseless endowment.

Most ideologies of the subject have been rooted in existential philosophy (hence their irritating and cumbersome psychologism). Bell's is among the first in architecture to free itself of these limitations, even if this has meant cultivating a new type of mysticism. For Bell, there is no existence that is not *social* existence, hence the centrality of the problem of the city in all of his work. No box is too simple or too rudimentary to reveal its roots in collective human activity—especially economic activity—nor too "basic," "formal," or "pure" to be seen as an agent of social action itself. In the 1960s and 1970s, subject formation theory in architecture was presented as a radical corrective to the aridity of modernist doctrine, a way to reconnect building to the conduct of public and private life. Architecture, it was naively surmised, makes us what we are. But in Bell's work the seemingly airless abstractions of modernism are seen not as things to overcome but rather to cultivate, exacerbate, and understand, for they already *are* us. For Bell, architecture does not *produce* subjectivity, it is already subject itself.

Bell is not interested in simply making objects that change the outcome of this or that all-too-human life. His goal is to produce subject-buildings that challenge our complacent beliefs about our own fashioning, our own subjectivity, our own relationship to the shaping forces of history. By making buildings that "have a life," he reminds us that we humans are not such special cases after all, that history (historical becoming) is something that we share with all organized matter and material life. Bell's architecture is not architecture at all (this is why it is so difficult to understand), but a form of extended urbanism (if one can grant that Augustine's *City of God* is this also) that borders on mystical cosmology (hence his claim that his primarily interest is to "broaden what architectural practice can address").

FIG 1 Glass House @
2 Degrees

1 Tactical inflections of
this type remained virtual
in the architectures of
Behrens and Mies.

Although I suggested that space held the equivalent position in Bell's universe that god held in that of many mystics, this formulation was incomplete. Because space is never presented in Bell's work as a distinct or definable thing, but as a regime of preexisting action that has itself been ceaselessly *transformed*. Following the work of the great economic historians of the last two centuries, space in Bell's work becomes a rationalized product of the action of money, that infinitely exchangeable, malleable, and protean invention of modern civilization. For Bell, the abandoning of the gold standard in 1971 serves as the constitutive event that gives birth to contemporary space. I am aware of no other architect practicing now or at any time in the past (aside from, perhaps, Moholy-Nagy, with his vision of a technically invested modern space entity) who has held such a radical and systematic theory of modern space. Bell's metaphysical project is to insist that all social transformation, however invisible or discrete, leaves its mark in the material world and at every scale. The great task is to reveal it.

What better way then to show the subtle, often infinitesimal, and maddeningly slow action of history on matter than through the steady, predictable box? And how else to explain the first use of the two-degree inflection (which refuses to be resolved in the cliché of curvature) in the history of architecture?[1] Similarly, Bell's fascination with the finite element analysis of Giuseppe Terragni (as well as with torsion, stress, and all other infinitesimal inflections) is really an argument about the mystical "participation" of economic flows within apparently resistant and static things. It is an undeniably strange but brilliant extension of a thermodynamic vision of matter (in many ways an architect's hyperbolic vision) that seeks to trace an infinitely disciplined curve so subtle and embedded that it never manifests itself in a line and requires different eyes in order to see. Molecules and capital, he argues, have a rich, secret, and especially entwined life whose conjugal mysteries can—indeed *must*—be revealed.

This is why the idiosyncratic primacy Bell gives to bizarre facts is easily justified. One may no longer underrate the importance of industrial process—how at one point in historical time, for example, light alloys (aluminum) came to replace steel. We are compelled today to go deep into the molecular record. For the metal matrixes and sensations embedded in our everyday routine emit information not only about the regimes of production *in which* we live, but far more basically, the regimes of production *of which* we are literally made. We are consubstantial with our world, inseparable from it, and by consequence too often blind to the pathways and regimens of creation that take place in it. Sometimes it requires a "mysticism" in order to break through and find new ways to listen and to see (think Stockhausen, Cage, Tarkovsky). Bell's boxes are transistors: it is their very *resistance* to ambient signals that endows them with their exquisite sensitivity to detect, filter, and channel significant change.

In House Inside Out: Space Replaces Us, Michael Bell sets out to "turn space inside out." His remarkable project, submitted as an entry to the Rem Koolhaas–judged House with No Style Competition, has the wildly ambitious motto "everywhere all at once." Bell's descriptive text, which reads like a Malevich-inspired science-fiction story, sets a tone of revolutionary reflection promising entry into the "true realm of modernity."

Problems of inside and outside are the essence of topology. (For a wonderful illustration of this simple definition, see the 1970 Charles and Ray Eames film on the subject.) Topology makes no distinction between a sphere and a torus, as each could be deformed or molded into the other. Once called "rubber sheet geometry," it has catapulted in prominence in recent years because of increased computational sophistication. New methods of understanding topology were used by Rene Thom in developing a general theory of biological form, which led to his disputed "catastrophe theory."

Fascinated by these mathematical and scientific aspects, Michael Bell is that rare architect who pushes architecture forward through real thought experiments. His father figures in the mysterious crossover zones that yield black-hole problems are John Hejduk and Robert Slutzky. And yet Bell is part of a new generation coming to bloom in the beginning of the twenty-first century—surely a century in which the computational speed of thought will project science and mathematics into fresh and exhilarating new thinking, but with what consequences for architecture?

I first came across Michael Bell's work when I was serving on the 1991 *Progressive Architecture* awards jury. Arriving late to the jury, which included Wolf Prix and Stanley Saitowitz, I found Bell's Double Dihedral House in the discarded pile. As anyone who has ever experienced the strange dynamics of an architectural jury knows, to reintroduce something from the rejects pile will incite agonizing controversy. (The same thing happened when Eero Saarinen arrived a day late to a 1957 jury; he chose Utzon's Sydney Opera House from the reject pile.) After considerable discussion, Bell's house and art gallery project for La Cienega, New Mexico, was given a top award. The way insides frame outsides and outsides frame insides gives this house a spatial reversibility in rectangular rhythms, condensed topological reflections.

I am always amazed at the poetic potential of the small house to collapse and densify an architectural thought. Bell's J-shaped house is the haiku of his initial phase of research. It is simply folded into itself, its only articulation being a bathroom and kitchen blocked out as tall masonry objects. (One thinks of Philip Johnson's description of his own glass house as "slipped over" the standing brick chimney of a war-burned house from his memory.) Bell writes, "If the skin belongs to space, then the building is a void—a hole in space—and the other edge of space comes into question."

Gaston Bachelard argued that a concept is truly scientific only to the extent that it becomes concrete by realization. Bell's work is both conceptual and material—even if not yet built, it creates concepts from material techniques and anticipates this reciprocal realization. We always ask an architect to build. Bachelard's American contemporary Thomas Kuhn wrote the barrier-breaking 1962 *The Structure of Scientific Revolutions*, which elevated the terms "paradigm," "paradigm change," and "paradigm shift" into nearly household words. Kuhn argued that scientists working under competing paradigms "live in different worlds." Architects like Michael Bell, driven by original thought experiments, likewise explore different worlds. Beyond mere expressionism and its fashionable curves, thought experiments in hybrid fields like science might lead us to the epistemological break necessary for twenty-first century architecture to deliver on its promise.

PROJECT CREDITS

Berlin (Topological) Stoa
Team : Marcus Meisner

Double Dihedral House
Thanks to: William Green

House Inside Out: Space Replaces Us
Team : Eric Hildebrant

Mathematics Day Care Center
Team: Jeff Kaeonil, Richard Winchell

Duration House
Team: Peony Quan, David Marini, Chris Nichols

Endspace: Michael Bell and Hans Hofmann
Team: Peony Quan, Ben Thorne, David Marini
Graphic Design: Sze Tsung Leong and Michael Bell
Steel Fabrication: George Secaris Studio, Houston, Texas
Funding: Lila Wallace-Reader's Digest Fund Museum
Accessibility Initiative
Special Thanks: Rice Advanced Visualization Lab (RAVL)

Chrome House
Team: Marc Swackhamer, Blair Satterfield, Lucia Chung

16 Houses: Owning a House in the City
Installation Design: Michael Bell and Kerry Whitehead
Steel Fabrication and Graphics: Kerry Whitehead
Installation Graphics: Gunar Hartmann, Logan Ray
Partner Organizations: DiverseWorks Artspace and Fifth Ward
Community Redevelopment Corporation
Visual Arts Director: Diane Barber, DiverseWorks Artspace
Assistant Curators: Mardie Oakes, Keith Krumweide
Construction Manager: Anna Mod
Advisory Committee: Jeff Balloutine, Bank United; Aaron
Betsky, Netherlands Architecture Institute; Rev. Clemons,
Fifth Ward Community Redevelopment Corporation; Farés
El Dahdah, Rice University; Stephen Fox, Anchorage Founda-
tion; Emily Todd, DiverseWorks Artspace; Robert Toliver,
Fifth Ward resident
Funding: Graham Foundation for Advanced Studies in the
Fine Arts; DiverseWorks Artspace; Cultural Arts Council
of Houston and Harris Counties; Local Initiatives Support
Corporation; Fifth Ward Community Redevelopment
Corporation; Rice University School of Architecture;
Bank United; and private donors

Glass House @ 2 Degrees
Team: John Mueller, Todd Vanvarick
Steel Consultant: Metalab, Houston

Stateless Housing
Urban Planning and Research: Michael Bell
Project Director: Michael Bell
Project Coordinator: Anthony Burke
Project Architects: Michael Bell Architecture,
Marble Fairbanks Architects, Mark Rakatansky
Studio Team: Kory Bieg, Nancy Bue, Glenn Fulk,
Jane Kim, Kaja Kuehl, Alexander Pfeiffer, Josh Uhl
Graphs of Income and Housing Types: Anthony Burke
Graphs of Concentration of HIV Infection and Relationship
Between Commuter Costs and Income: Jane Kim and
Glenn Fulk
Photograph of NYC Housing Authority Hallway: Kaja Kuehl

Stations House
Team: Thomas Long

Binocular House
Team: Thomas Long
Associate Architect: Stephen O'Dell
Structural Engineer: Robert Silman Associates, P.C.
Mechanical Engineer: Altieri Sebor Wieber LLC
Landscape Architect: Margie Ruddick Landscape
Contractor: Mitchell Rabideau